How
Children
Learn to
write

John W.A. Smith

Warwick B. Elley

Richard C. Owen Publishers, Inc.
Katonah, New York

Preface

In this book we have set out to help classroom teachers tease out from the many competing viewpoints some defensible positions about the best way to introduce children to writing. Although we see this book as a companion to *Learning to Read in New Zealand* (1994) we are the first to admit that the research on children's writing occupies a Cinderella position – when compared with research on reading. Writing may be the second 'r' but we have to recognise that as teachers we have all wandered in the wilderness of ignorance for far too long. Generations of students have grown up with a distaste for – even a fear of – writing, and have done all they can to avoid it in later life. This is a serious admission, and one which we as authors wish to address.

The recent introduction of the Process Writing movement and the new developments in Cognitive Theory, Linguistic Theory and Applied Behaviour Analysis have thrown up a number of exciting ideas which have significant implications for teachers. Their appearance on the scene coincides with a need, felt by many teachers, to justify their practices to an increasingly sophisticated community of parents who want to know why their children are exposed to educational experiences which are different from the ones they had when they were at school.

If we have been able to help some teachers develop a consistent philosophy, based on relevant research and diverse experience, we will be pleased. If some interested parents are also able to gain new insights into their children's growth in written language, we will be even more delighted.

The authors of this book bring long years of relevant experience to their writing. One has been involved in teacher training and language curriculum issues for some 30 years; the other has over 40 years' experience in research, teaching and assessment, chiefly in literacy, and has worked in New Zealand and in a number of other countries. Both of us have studied children learning to read and write, and have tried to acquaint ourselves with current theories and recent research findings. We do not have all the answers, and much more remains to be done. Perhaps we should regard this book as a stage along the way. Certainly we have grown in the writing of it, and learned to appreciate in the process the wisdom behind E. M. Forster's classic maxim – 'How do I know what I think until I see what I say?'

No book is ever the sole creation of its authors. We wish to thank our ever-patient wives for tolerating our absences, both in body and in mind – and our tendency to an excessive preoccupation with the contents which follow. We are indebted also to Professor Ted Glyn who showed us the role that modern applied behaviour analysis plays in education, to many colleagues at the Dunedin College of Education who endured an interrogation from one of the authors as they had a crumpled draft chapter pushed before them, to Gail Morris and Michael Wi for assistance with word processing, to Shelley Frew who patiently tracked down the most obscure references, and to Marnie Scott, Joan Turner and Jeanette Elley who shared with us the delights of their young children's early writing.

Contents

Introduction

CHAPTER 1

'If you wish to be a writer, write.'

Epictetus, (110 AD) Discourses II

This book describes how children best learn to write in schools. Learning to write is a part of the school curriculum beset by claims and counter-claims from pressure groups. When should children begin to write? How often should they write? Who should choose the topic? How do they learn to spell? Which is best, teaching grammar directly or letting children write what they like and allowing the grammar to sort itself out? How should writing be assessed, how often, and by whom? Can we afford to ignore their faults? How can we best help our pupils?

Too often the findings of systematic research are lost in the cries of claims and counter-claims. Today's teachers must be able to articulate, not only their philosophy of teaching, but also the underlying evidence for that philosophy. 'Parents, and society in general, are demanding higher levels of professionalism from teachers, and it is now expected that teachers will be able to articulate their teaching beliefs' (Hood, 1995, p. 4). It is true that many competent teachers cannot cite the research findings which underlie their approach to the teaching of writing. This is a dangerous position for a profession. Doctors who do not understand the actions of drugs on the body, lawyers who do not understand the law, accountants who do not change their practices in accordance with changes in tax rulings, these professionals go out of business rapidly. Why should the teaching profession be any different?

Why write?

People write for a variety of reasons. Poetry and stories express our emotions, lists remind us what to buy at the supermarket, instructions tell people what to do, letters keep us in touch. But for children and tertiary students alike, writing is the prime means of demonstrating to others that they have learned something – from a five-year-old's account of a visit from Gran, to a 30-year-old's doctoral dissertation on the Argentinian stem weevil. In these instances the products will differ markedly but the processes used to produce the final products are similar. Some thinking has to have occurred; thoughts are then translated into a form of language and then are expressed on paper. Along the way, conventions are invoked by the writer – word sequencing, letter formation, spelling, grammar, layout. These processes influence and in turn are influenced by the content. And there is a constant influence from other people – a teacher, classmates who read a draft or look over the writer's shoulder. There is a continual interaction between the writer's ideas and their expression, and this interaction modifies both the expression and the ideas.

Little wonder then, that for many people writing is a difficult task and has never ranked highly in surveys of subjects children enjoy at school (see Chapter 5).

Nevertheless, many children learn to write – and to enjoy writing – as they move through school. So we begin this book with some examples of one child's writing gathered over a period of five years. She is an articulate child, eager to express her thoughts on paper. We will return to her writing, and to that of others, throughout the book.

Here is Katy writing at age 5, just after she has started school. It is a remarkable piece of writing. A succinct message is conveyed. She assumes the reader will understand that her cat is called 'Rodney'

Katy at 5 years

I Love cats
My cats
Rodny .

and does not need to write that 'Rodney' is a name, not a breed of cat. There is a mixture of capital letters and no punctuation. The drawing is an integral part of the writing and preceded it. At this stage, for Katy writing is simply talking drawn on paper.

A year later, at age 6, Katy's Rodney is still the centre of Katy's writing and probably still of her affections. There is still a drawing, but this time there is a sun and sky as well as Rodney. She has written 19 words, all spelt correctly.

She has learned about capital letters, and that they are used when things are named. This learning has been interpreted to mean that all nouns are capitalised – a generous interpretation of the rules of capitalisation. Her sentence structure has become more elaborate with 'and' joining three clauses to the opening statement. In addition she has used 'her' to make the story cohesive where previously she may have repeated 'Rodney'.

At seven, Katy has left Rodney behind as a subject, although she is

Katy at 6 years

This is my Cat and
her Name is RodNey
and I Love her
and I take Care
of her and

Katy at 7 years

Today I went to the
dentist. She said that I
was perfict. I got two
staps and a sticer

still writing about her own experiences. A more complex story demonstrates that the basic idea of a sentence has been understood. Spelling mistakes suggest that she is venturing into the more unfamiliar territory of complex words that she may not have already encountered in her reading books. We can also discern a developing understanding of the complex relationship between letters and sounds. There is no picture. The story stands by itself.

A year later, at age 8, Katy's writing is such that we can read a coherent piece of imaginative writing. Her sentence structure uses a range of constructions (conditional: 'If I was...' tentativeness: 'I think there will...') with accurate punctuation.

Her spelling shows she is aware of the intricacies of spelling, even if she has not yet mastered traditional orthography. 'Abell' and 'keahole' represent valiant attempts at 'able' and 'keyhole'. Her writing is given a title.

By age 9, Katy's writing has taken another leap forward and shows the effects of her wide reading and love of books. The writing uses constructions and vocabulary usually found only in writing ('It was day thirteen' 'there was a lull').

Direct speech makes its appearance. The construction builds tension into the story and the reader wonders what the climax will be. And after all, if it was good enough for Sendak's Max to escape from the Wild Things by sailing away and waking up in his own bed, then it is good enough for Katy to escape from the terrible storm by being knocked out and waking up safely on an island.

> **Katy at 8 years**
>
> The Locked room   8 yrs
>
> If I was looking through a Keahole of a locked room I would be abell to see all The old Junk from The Samarly and a wardrobe full of all the christmes stuf. I would see fat spider on a tiny spider web. I would see all the Old Broken rugs and matchreses and all the old toys. I Think there will be a cat with babies in the room.

> **Katy at 9 years**
>
> The Nightmare
>
> It was day thirteen on our trip to the Indies we wer in the midelill of the pacifac ocean the suddenly there was a lull every thing stoped there was complete silence then the storm broke there was lightning and clouds everywhere then suddenly. I heard a crack and saw the mast fall down right before my very eyes. the captain shouted "every-body dow below" and that was all I knew because I was knocked out when I woke up we were all safe on the Island.

Katy at 10 years

Biography!

On September the 4th Amelia Brown
was brought into the world. Amelia brought
lots of Happiness to the pround perents
Louise and Andrew Brown and jealousey
to two older odoped brothers. after
two days she was brought home to the
new house at 136 grange Rd
As they used to live in wellington.
eight months later she grew her first
teeth. When she was five, she started
school.and she did well because she
liked her so much. Her teachers
name was Mrs Jones

When Amelia grows up she wants to
be a obstetrician and a pediatrician
She does not want to get married or
have children. Amelia's hobbies are
baby sitting and playing netball. When

Summer in Auckland means
there will be some disisadvantage
and lots of advantages. My
favourit advantage is going swimming
because I am really good at it
and my worst one is when you are
so hot you get very bored
and that is called boredom.
You can get very sunburt if you
do not put on any sun block.

Finally, we present two pieces of writing completed when Katy was 10. The narrative shows more signs of wider reading and she uses the vocabulary that she thinks adults would use ('was brought into this world'; 'when she turned 9...'; 'brought lots of happiness'). The mechanical aspects of writing (spelling and punctuation) have been mastered, and we can perhaps interpret the occasional spelling or punctuation error more to haste than to lack of knowledge.

The second piece is an exposition and again demonstrates a remarkable degree of sophistication in linking two concepts – summer and boredom.

In five years, Katy has progressed from being able to write brief utterances to a writer of fluent prose able to use a range of genre. To understand how this has happened, we will draw upon many sources of information in this book – and will consider the complex interplay between home, parents, teachers and the school curriculum that have helped Katy to become a literate person.

The organisation of this book

This book begins with a general discussion of children's language development, and its relation to thought and writing. It outlines the efforts of young children in their first scribblings. Then it describes a number of viewpoints on how writing is learned at school. Next, controversial issues, such as the teaching of grammar and spelling, are addressed. Finally, we outline a working synthesis which represents our current view on how we can best help children to write.

More specifically, in Chapter 2 we have set out to briefly describe recent research on children's thinking, language and development and the role schools and society play in that development. We consider also the differences between language used for talking and language that is written down. Chapter 3 outlines beginning writing. We look at pre-schoolers' first tentative attempts at writing, while Chapter 4 describes progress made during the first two years at school. Chapter 5 describes traditional approaches which have been used to teach writing in our schools in the past.

The next five chapters consider some new, non-traditional approaches to studying how children learn to write. Chapter 6 draws on the work of Donald Graves, and describes the 'process' approach which is used by whole language advocates. It must now be considered to be the dominant theory in New Zealand and much of North America. A similar approach, which is popular in Australia, is described in the work of Brian Cambourne discussed in Chapter 7. Chapter 8 is based upon the work of cognitive psychologists. The contribution behaviourist theory has made to our understanding of how to foster the development of writing skills is described in Chapter 9. The wider role of writing across the curriculum is described in Chapter 10. The role of grammar is considered in Chapter 11 and the learning of spelling in Chapter 12. The effects of technologies on learning to write in a rapidly changing world is examined in Chapter 13. Developmental descriptions of the characteristics of writing at different phases are set out in Chapter 14. The complex issue of assessment is discussed in Chapter 15. Our final chapter pulls the disparate threads from the previous chapters together to a workable synthesis for teachers.

Gathering knowledge about writing: a note on methodology

Writing is difficult to study in the abstract – and this book is an abstraction. Writing is always about something – about dinosaurs, or about my first kiss, or about how I foiled the drug barons. Writing is easier to do, than to write about. Introspection about the process is difficult, artificial and can be unreliable.

Researchers use a variety of methods to gain dependable knowledge about children's writing. Each of these methods has its own strengths and weaknesses. As none of them is likely to provide the full picture, we prefer to adopt the position that each can offer something useful to enhance our understanding of the best way to help children to improve their writing.

Table 1 sets out a list of the most common research strategies referred to in this book, along with some examples and brief comments on their major strengths and limitations.

Method	Examples	Strengths	Limitations
1 Surveys of pupil performance Large samples are assessed under standardised conditions.	IEA writing survey of pupil writing in 15 countries (chapter 5).	• Reveals what a cross-section of pupils can do. • Writing produced under standardised conditions. • Can show relationships with environmental factors.	• One-off writing may not be typical for some. • Focus on product not process. • Time-consuming to assess.
2 Surveys of pupil attitudes/strategies Large samples are observed or questioned by interview or questionnaire.	• Harry Hood's survey of 100 pupils in Southland NZ (chapter 6).	• Reveals how a cross-section of pupils think or behave. • Can produce a large amount of data quickly. • Can show relationships with environmental factors.	• Expressed attitudes may not be honest. • Unsuitable with young children.
3 Controlled experiments Classroom experiments in which new methods are compared with those of control groups undergoing traditional instruction.	• Bereiter and Scardamalia's studies in Toronto (chapter 8). • Elley et al. experiment on teaching of grammar (chapter 11).	• Can show effects of a strategy or method of instruction on children's writing skill or attitudes.	• Difficult to control all variables. • Writing exercises may be artificial or atypical.
4 Applied behavioural experiments Pupils' environment is systematically varied to investigate effects on their responses.	• Glynn's studies of pupils in Auckland and Dunedin (chapter 10).	• Can show effects of systematically controlled changes in environment on children's behaviour or attitudes.	• Confined to small samples. • May be seen as artificial.
5 Case studies Single cases or small groups are studied closely under typical conditions.	• Graves' studies of progress of individual pupils under process writing (chapter 6). • Flower and Hayes's studies of mature writers (chapter 8).	• Allows in-depth analysis of children's thinking and writing. • Graphic descriptions often more persuasive for practitioners.	• Confined to small numbers which may not be typical. • Difficult to generalise to other pupils.
6 Correlation studies Assessment procedures compared for validity; surveys show relationship between writing and other variables.	• Comparisons of holistic and analytic grading (chapter 14).	• Reveals patterns in data which lead to better policy. • Shows trends which suggest closer study by other methods.	• Cannot show cause-and-effect relationships. • Requires large samples to produce stable results.

Table 1 *– Major research methods for studying writing*

Two of the common research methods deal with **surveys of many students** in many schools. Thus 500 students may write essays on a given topic, and respond to questionnaires about their home and school circumstances. This approach has the distinct advantage of showing the full picture, rather than what is characteristic of a small number of enthusiasts or abnormal cases. But surveys usually lack depth. They can report what students can do, or typically say, under certain standard conditions, but they cannot get below the surface. Questionnaires completed by hundreds of participants are seldom as revealing as interviews with individuals or observations of classrooms at work. Students' responses to questions about attitudes may not be honest assessments of their typical beliefs. Nor are their teachers necessarily any more accurate. And if 500 students are required to write a one-off essay for a research study, it may, or may not, be typical of what they could do if they were choosing the topic, or writing for an authentic purpose. Nevertheless, surveys can reveal problem areas for further study, or policy action, particularly when they show negative attitudes and practices, or indicate unexpected talents or unsuspected inequalities.

Controlled experiments have the potential to show that one approach is more effective than another in improving children's writing, but the method is fraught with traps for the uninitiated. For instance, if the comparisons are to be fair, the participants in both (or all) methods should be similar in relevant respects (age, ability, attitudes); the teachers of both groups should be similar in competence, and give the competing methods similar amounts of time and emphasis; the assessments of writing should not favour one group over the other – and so on. When the differences in outcomes are large, the researcher can be confident that the superior method would be better for other students in other schools, but it usually takes several such studies to confirm such a conclusion – and the studies should preferably be conducted at different grade levels, and in different socio-economic districts.

Researchers who favour an **applied behaviour analysis** prefer to operate on single individuals or small groups. Under such circumstances, they can systematically vary those aspects of the classroom environment (praise, type of feedback) which they believe will affect pupils' writing behaviour or attitudes. Often this approach can reveal important findings as Chapter 9 will show. Again, it usually takes a number of time-consuming, carefully controlled studies before generalisations which are useful for teachers can be agreed upon.

The case study is one of several 'ethnographic' research methods which are designed to investigate individual students, or classes, or institutions – without any systematic attempt to alter them, but rather to reveal how they work. Case studies usually use observation methods, interviews and analysis of children's writing in an attempt to understand the complexity of factors which make them what they are. They do not start with specific hypotheses, and the reports from case studies are usually narrative or anecdotal, but should be 'bounded' by the aim of the research. They often produce unexpected insights, which may be of immediate benefit for teachers or researchers. However, they are usually confined to small numbers, making it difficult to draw general conclusions without further study. Donald Graves' research, and that of others in the process writing camp, make effective use of case studies (see Chapter 6). Interview studies conducted by Flower and Hayes of writers reporting their thought processes as they write, are further examples (see Chapter 8).

Correlational studies are designed to reveal patterns in large bodies of data, collected from many students. Thus, a survey study may show a high correlation between two kinds of grading policies, but low correlations with a third. Another study may show that the number of hours students spend reading and writing correlates more highly with writing ability in the lower primary school than they do with older students. Such findings may require closer analysis and frequently suggest policy change. Correlations can reveal links between teaching procedures and student behaviour, but they cannot reveal why such links exist. We cannot argue from correlation to causation, without conducting further studies to isolate the causal factors. Sometimes A causes B, sometimes B causes A, and sometimes both are affected by a third unsuspected factor C, which is the real cause.

All these approaches, and variations on them, have a place in revealing the secrets of children's writing development, and all are referred to and used in generating our opinions and conclusions in this book.

A personal note

The two authors bring to this book complementary backgrounds, one in curriculum studies and the other in educational psychology with some emphasis on assessment techniques. We believe that these backgrounds provide some interesting tools to study writing, but at the same time they can give us only a partial picture of what is happening. In analysing writing, the sum of the whole is always greater than the parts. Effective writing, like reading, is more than just the cumulative effect of vocabulary, syntax, style, intent, clarity, voice. A piece of writing can have an interesting vocabulary, well organised content, acceptable use of syntax, elegant style and purpose and yet still be boring and unclear to its intended reader. Even if we could define 'perfect' writing there is no guarantee that anyone would want to read it when we'd produced it. Perhaps we could think of successful writing as a transaction which takes place between writer and reader. If the writing is to be good, the transaction must be successful. The writer adds to the knowledge, emotions and attitudes the reader brings to the printed page. The reader has learned something from the writer.

We don't have all the answers. Our understanding of how we learn to write is still beset by claim and counter-claim from researchers and practitioners. We have tried to assemble in this book recent thinking and research to reveal insights into how children learn to write. But the complete picture still lacks some details and each of the differing research paradigms illuminates the researchers' own corner of theory or an aspect of practice. Indeed, the process of a complete description of how children learn to write is similar to the group of blind men describing an elephant. Each thought the part he held represented the complete animal – hence the man who felt a tusk thought the animal was smooth and hard; the men who held the ear thought it was floppy; the men who felt a leg thought it was round and tall, while the man who held the tail felt it was like a fly whisk. And no description of the elephant's physical attributes described the elephant's personality. We have attempted to provide a more complete picture in our book than the blind men were able to!

Thinking, speaking and writing

'Spoken thoughts come freely in the school yard, but written ones are laboured in the classroom.'

A. Silberman, (1991) Growing Up Writing

 Thought into language

The basis of all writing is thought. We think before we write, and we think as we write. On the surface it would be easy to say that writing merely involves putting our thoughts down on paper. Like all simplistic definitions, however, this teaches us little. The difficulty is that we know all too little about how the mind processes and stores our thoughts. There is no simple linear relationship between words and thoughts. The influential Russian psychologist Vygotsky (1962) referred to thought as 'inner speech'. Whether that speech is in a form that we would recognise as the everyday currency of speech is open to debate. Inner speech has been described as 'a dynamic, unstable thing, fluttering between word and thought' (Vygotsky, 1962, p. 149).

Can we really think without words? Some thoughts are undoubtedly verbal, but others are images, emotions or sensations, not easily expressed in words. For example, we have far more words for colour than we have for taste. Yet we are all aware of fine gradations of taste when we eat – particularly if we are travelling and eating unusual food. Or consider the difficulty of describing a dream to another person. We are all aware that in the process of telling about the dream we are not quite capturing in words what exactly happened and how we felt about it. Likewise, some school topics are difficult to describe in words. Could we learn geometry without diagrams, or appreciate music without listening to the melody?

Philosophers often speculate on how we shape thought into words, at the point of utterance (Britton, 1983). For some it is a laborious process entailing fastidious preparation of background knowledge, listing of helpful vocabulary, trial, error, and thorough revision. For fluent writers it 'just happens'. This is probably because the whole process has become automatic, through repeated practice.

Vygotsky (1962) claims that thought and language begin as separate entities. Babies, after all, appear to think long before they can speak. But as they grow, thought and language gradually become entwined and inseparable. Vygotsky writes that 'at about the age of two the curves of development of thought and speech, till then separate, meet and join to initiate a new form of behaviour' (p. 43). This new form of behaviour, according to Vygotsky, occurs when speech begins to serve the intellect.

He goes on to suggest that 'thought development is determined by language' (p. 51) which in its turn is developed by the tools of linguistics and sociocultural experiences. These include, for today's children, not only conversations but also books and stories, films and television. Thus, thoughts depend on linguistic abilities, which in turn are dependent on interactions with the society around us. For Vygotsky, children learn firstly through interactions with the people around them, and when these learnings have been internalised, from their own thoughts and mental drives.

Flower and Hayes (1984) suggest that meanings have many representations and that the work of the writer is to translate these meanings into one medium, into prose. It would be tempting to argue that all that needs to happen is for the representations of meaning to be transformed into words which are in turn written down, but as the following section will show, writing is more than just talk written down.

Compared with the abstract notions of cognitive psychologists and philosophers in their efforts to unravel the mysteries of thought, speech is relatively easy to understand. But even if the child becomes competent at translating his or her images and experiences into words, there is still the further problem to be solved of recording these words on paper. Most children learn to speak effortlessly, without teachers and certainly without an elaborate structure of preschools and schools to support them. The only exceptions are the few children born deaf or who suffer severe deprivation as young children. The rest learn speech without having to really try. We interact with the people in our environment about things that amuse us, intrigue us, excite us or puzzle us.

Writing is a not a universal phenomenon. Many societies have never developed a writing system and their language exists only in an oral form. Where a writing system has developed, many people are unable to use it. Stubbs (1980) estimates that 40% of the world's population cannot read, and a further 25% cannot use their writing system for any significant purposes. Nor is writing the most common form of language expression. Kress (1994, p. 17) estimates that for every word written, a hundred thousand are spoken. Nevertheless, writing is an essential skill for all who would live, and work, and raise a family, and participate in a modern community.

How do young children learn to speak?

As babies, we learn language to make sense of our world. Sacks (1995) expressed the meaning-making aspect of language vividly when he wrote 'We are not given our world; we make our world through incessant experience, categorization and reconnection'.

Language is the medium which refines and shapes our creation of the world we experience. In this sense, everyone's mental picture of the world is unique.

We learn to speak through our interactions with other people in our environment. A detailed discussion of language acquisition is beyond the scope of this book. We will confine ourselves here to commenting on several aspects of language development that have particular implications for learning to write.

1 It is widely accepted by linguists that **humans are born with an innate predisposition to speak** – we are the only species that can communicate freely with each other. Psychologists have laboured long and at great expense to teach other species to communicate with oral language but have had little success.

2 **Our speech is developed and refined through interactions with people around us** who provide models for our syntax and enrich our vocabularies. If the speech patterns of our first models are different from those of school teachers, then we will have difficulty adjusting to the school's expectations.

3 **We learn our language by using it, and by receiving feedback about the success of its use**. A young child seeing a four-legged creature that barks will say 'doggie' and his parents will approve with comments like 'Isn't he clever?' But when the child sees a four-legged creature that meows and he says 'doggie', his parents will respond – 'No, that's a cat'. So their response to his utterance is usually based on the truth of the statement, on its meaning. Parents generally focus more on children's language content than on its form. The research we will review suggests that in this respect, learning to write has clear parallels with learning to speak.

4 **Formal instruction plays little part in learning to speak one's native language**. Most of one's native language is acquired incidentally in real life contexts. Successful use of language serves to meet the child's needs. In fact, formal instruction is often counter-productive. Again, there are parallels in learning to write. Tough (1974, p. 56) demonstrated the futility of trying to impose an adult grammar on a young child with the following observation of a dialogue at an English nursery school:

TOMMY:	'Can I have the scissors?'
MISS H:	'May I have the scissors, *please*, Miss H?'
TOMMY:	'I want some scissors'
MISS H:	'Well, then you must say: "May I have the scissors please, Miss H." 'Let me hear you say that.'
TOMMY:	'Can I–'
MISS H:	'May I – now.'
TOMMY:	'May I – can I have the scissors?'
MISS H:	'Oh, Tommy, say "please".'
TOMMY:	'Please – the scissors.'

Tommy is trying to get his request heard. He wants the scissors. The teacher is more concerned with getting Tommy to use a particular form of polite speech than with giving him the scissors. What is happening is that the teacher is focusing on the surface features of the utterance while the child is concerned with the substance of the utterance. It is hard for the child to cope with both. One can only admire Tommy's persistence. All he wants is a pair of scissors. He is getting an ineffective lesson in speech.

5 **Children's speech has its own grammar**. Although that grammar may differ from an adult grammar, it is nonetheless a grammar system with its own consistent conventions. So when the young child says 'We goed to the shop', we realise that the child has over-generalised from his/her understanding that events that happened in the past have -*ed* added to the end to signify past happenings. Unfortunately, English has many exceptions to its rule structure. It will be some time before that child learns that we use 'went' instead of the logical 'goed'. So children do seek patterns in language use, and try to follow those patterns in their oral language production. The same can be said of their efforts in written language.

It is tempting to think, then, that writing is just speech with an overlay of graphemes (written letters) and spelling, just 'speech written down'. In fact, there are many differences between our typical spoken and written language. It is worthwhile to reflect on these differences, as spelt out below. These differences help us to understand why many children find writing difficult.

 ## Differences between speech and writing

1 We speak in continuous streams of phonemes, but we write in separate words. So young children have to learn that words are separate entities with gaps between them. Linguists who analyse flows of speech find that pause boundaries often do not necessarily coincide with word boundaries. For instance, 'west end' is usually pronounced 'wes tend' by most people; 'look out' is said as one word. Again, the written words are organised into sentences, which is an issue only in writing. We frequently speak in fragments (*Look here! What on earth?*) or in incomplete sentences. Nobody objects to this practice.

2 Writing depends on learning conventions of spelling, punctuation, capital letters and paragraphs – which have no direct counterpart in speech. For many children, with little exposure to print, these conventions do become a major challenge.

3 Speech occurs in a context with another person present. Frank Smith (1982) argues that this is a far more important distinction between speech and writing than the obvious point that speech is aural and writing is visual. Conversations usually take place between people who know each other. The listener can provide prompts or cues and respond to the utterances. The listener's cues guide and stimulate the speaker to continue.

Writing, however, offers no such cues. For example, the utterance 'Would you like another cup?' would be interpreted differently depending on whether the conversation is taking place in a coffee shop, in a china shop or at a sports prize-giving ceremony. The language and the situation are indivisible. The one cannot be understood without the other. Once we know the context, relevant cues can be picked up which allow the utterance to be understood more easily. And if the speech is not understood, the listener can ask for clarification. In writing, however, the writer has to imagine the presence of the reader, to predict the reader's needs, and provide additional information accordingly.

4   Gesture and intonation play a key role in speech, for which capitals and punctuation marks form only a poor substitute. Except for occasional pictorial illustrations and subtleties of layout, there are no additional cues for establishing meaning. They have to be acquired, unaided, from the text. The writer has to supply the context. For example, 'Cut off a stick about this long, and hold it up like this', has little meaning in print. And an utterance such as 'Fred likes Susie' will be interpreted differently by the listener depending on whether the speaker's emphasis is placed on *likes* or on *Susie*. Where it is placed on 'likes' the listener may be meant to understand that it is surprising that Fred's feelings towards Susie may be more than just that of a simple acquaintance; where the emphasis is on 'Susie' the implication is that it is Susie who is an object of affection, rather than Charlene. To convey these nuances of meaning in writing may require more than just one sentence – as this attempt at explication has just shown!

5   Speech is more informal and strung out; writing is more formal and condensed. There is a high level of redundancy in speech which is marked also by pauses and 'fillers' such as 'well' or 'you know' or even a range of 'ums' or 'ahs'. Speech uses more contractions, slang, oaths and swear words. By contrast, writing is marked by a higher number of content words, more abstractions, more variety in verb tenses, and fewer fillers. Nervous lecturers who carefully write out the entire text of their lecture verbatim before delivering it, will lose their audience quickly because the spoken material is usually too dense for their listeners to comprehend easily. Consider also the narrator's use of 'Little did they know that...' and 'Nor did he realise that...', phrases found only in writing.

6   Writing is used to record the serious events of life. Wills are written, not tape-recorded; financial reports, government policies and legal documents are recorded in print. Shopping lists and the minutes of meetings are also best recorded in writing or print. However, speech can convey far better than writing the emotional aspects of life. Spoken declarations of love can convey subtleties of meaning, desires and expectations missing in even the most eloquent love-letter. Passionately held political agendas and religious messages are most convincing when they are spoken. Gossip is best left unrecorded.

7   Speech is transitory. Unless an audio recording is made, speech is lost

once it has been uttered. Writing is usually permanent and therefore has to be more carefully planned and crafted. It can also be revised, whereas speech can not. Words said in conversation remain spoken, and cannot be recalled by the speaker. The next utterance can be modified, depending on the listener's reaction, but the words themselves cannot be unsaid.

8   Writing is more tiring to produce than speech, is produced more slowly and makes greater demands on self-control and memory. Frank Smith points out that an average reader operates at 200–300 words per minute; a writer at 25 words per minute. Complex muscular movements are required which children often find difficult to sustain for long periods. By contrast, speech requires little physical effort from the speaker. Horowitz and Newman (cited in Perera, 1994, p. 161) estimate that it requires six minutes of writing to produce one minute of speech. To produce the writing, the writer not only has to remember the content, but also the conventions required for acceptable spelling, handwriting, punctuation and grammar. In speech, patterns of utterances acceptable to the listener require little conscious effort on the part of the speaker.

9   Writing is more often reviewed and subjected to judgements and assessment – speech is not. We often say: 'you have made a spelling mistake here and this section could be expressed more clearly' in response to a piece of writing. We seldom say to a speaker 'you mumbled when you asked if you could borrow the car and you didn't pronounce the final "t" in "tonight".'

10   The reader has control over the amount read and the ways in which the written information is absorbed. The reader can skim, read word by word, re-read or omit chunks, whereas a listener does not have the same control over the way information is presented. Listening is a linear process but reading provides the reader with the possibility of darting all over the text and not processing the print in the sequential way that the writer intended.

There are other differences between speech and writing that help underline the point that they are not parallel skills. However, enough has been said to illustrate that learning to write presents a greater challenge than learning to speak.

Summary

It is difficult to separate thought from language, and Vygotsky believes that from the age of two, thought and language are almost impossible to separate. Language is a vehicle for thought. However, although speaking and writing both use language, they are not mirror images of each other. The chosen medium requires adjustments – usually made unconsciously by native speakers. It is wrong to say that one medium is better than another.

Both serve different purposes and both have their own conventions to be observed by the user. While there are apparently more challenges to be faced in learning to write, there is nothing to suggest that they cannot be overcome by using similar methods to those used when faced with the challenge of learning to speak.

Perera (1994, p. 200) sums up the difference between the two modes thus:

'Conversation is typically spontaneous, informal, ephemeral and interactive; most often it takes place between people who know each other. The language is supported by both non-verbal communication and by the situational context... The most distinctive characteristics of writing are that it is planned, organised and durable; it is not bound to any physical setting and is frequently read by people unknown to the author.'

Early writing **3**

'Literacy begins at home'

Canadian Postage Stamp, (1996)

The beginnings of writing are established long before children attend school and receive formal instruction in writing. This chapter describes the writing children do before they go to school, and then places it in a theoretical context. The emergent writing of three children – Hannah, Callum and Rory – will be examined. Then, their development is explained theoretically, using the concepts of Vygotsky and of McNaughton. Finally, a study by McNaughton et al. (1996) discusses the writing of six families six months before the children began school.

Leaving your mark

Young children enjoy making marks on paper that remain after they have finished the physical act of drawing. Marks are made not only on paper but also on walls, books, table-cloths – virtually anything that can retain marks. Today a range of materials is available for children to write on – from post-it notes which can be written on and temporarily attached to any surface, to whiteboards that stick to refrigerator doors with magnets, as well as writing paper, newsprint and books, with and without lines. A variety of tools can be used to make marks – from pencils, pens, crayons, felt-tip markers and paint to less conventional tools. Goodridge (Goodridge and McNaughton, 1993) has described children using sand and mud to make messages while McNaughton (1995) describes a mother's observations of a child making letters with water on the concrete path outside the home. One of our case study children, Hannah, drew with coloured chalk on the concrete paths around her house when she was just over a year old. Not surprisingly, then, one of the difficulties in studying early writing is that much of it is dismissed as 'scribbling' and ignored or thrown away by parents.

Right from the start, children expect others to make sense of the marks they make. The writer's job is seen as producing the marks on the page while the reader's task is to provide a meaning for them. 'Tell me what I wrote.'

Here, for instance, is Callum's letter to Kim, written when he was only two years and three months.

It 'was about the holidays,' he told his mother – but she was expected to provide an explicit message. His brother, at about the same age, would 'write' by drawing, cutting and pasting on the same page. Rory saw writing as a multi-media production to create a world with none of the adult distinctions between drawing and forming letters operating. Reading the message was the province of older people who knew how to turn marks into sounds. Meaning was not considered by the writer as fixed in place by the text, but was a function of the reader. However, within five years – by the time they are seven – both boys will be able to write coherent stories which can be read by other people. How has this remarkable progression been achieved? How do they learn to write? Do they all pass through the same stages? What do they need to be told? How much do they teach themselves?

Callum's letter to Kim

To attempt to answer these questions, we need to examine Vygotsky's theory of language development (1962). Vygotsky was a Russian psychologist, whose writings about children's thinking and language development have made a substantial impact on our current views about children's learning. He is often referred to as a *social constructivist*. That is, he believed that children construct their own knowledge of the world as a result of their individual interactions with their social and cultural environment. There is no objective reality to be grasped. Rather, we make our own conceptions of the world, and each of us has a unique picture of it. One child's construction of writing as an activity is different from the next's, depending on his/her conception of it.

Vygotsky and society

All learning takes place in two stages – first the individual learns from the society around her (inter-individual), and then changes take place within the individual (intra-individual).

From birth we are part of society. In the preschooler's growing mastery of writing we can observe the myriad family interactions that foster literacy growth. Callum, Rory and Hannah have had stories read to them from infancy so links between print, picture and story have been clearly established. They are building up their individual mental constructions which correspond to their perceptions of experiences. In each family, children would see their parents writing in the evening. Hannah, as a young child, would ask, 'What are you doing?' and when told that her mother/father was writing would reply, 'Then I'm going to write too'. Callum writes his letter to Kim while sitting next to his mother who is also writing to Kim. Preschool teachers write children's names on their paintings and often write to record the child's dictated comments on their pictures.

Of course, Vygotsky's concept of 'society' has wider connotations than the immediate family. To the world of siblings, parents, and grand-parents, we must add the world of school, of work, of entertainment, or signs in the environment, for these too employ both reading and writing. Our definition of the social world of the child has to be inclusive of the wider society. During visits to her father's workplace, Hannah usually occupies herself by writing and drawing on office paper. Rory's attempts at early writing are influenced not only by his mother's writing but also by Callum's school-related activities, to the point where Rory, after observing some of the school demands for 'correctness' in writing, will only write if it is spelt correctly.

Society's cultural festivals also impact on young children's writing. Christmas is not only heralded by demands for presents but for many children it is a time of list writing – an order form for Santa. Callum wants 12 cars. His mother modelled and helped him write his list. Clearly, much of what he understands by reading and writing is the result of his social interactions. The web of meanings children attach to literacy activities is individual, derived from their own unique experiences with books and writing, and the people who introduce them to this new world. It is important that these experiences be positive ones, from the outset.

Callum's Christmas list (1)

Vygotsky and language

Vygotsky considered that language was a tool allowing us to act upon the world by mediation. To use Vygotsky's example, a knot tied in a handkerchief to remind us of something is a sign or a mediation. Words are mediators that allow us to manipulate things in the abstract. If my friends want to get from the airport to my house I can use words to tell them how to get here. I don't have to drive out and personally show them the way. Words give substance to the mental images of the road that I hold in my head. These same words mediate another set of (hopefully similar) images in my friends' heads.

Young children develop language to allow them to act upon the world more easily. A baby cries until she is given a bottle of milk; as she gets older experience tells her that she can point to the bottle (pointing is a mediation) to get fed. Soon she discovers that words are more effective than pointing, and the words 'milk' or 'drink' are usually suitably rewarded. Language becomes a way of structuring thought. Hunger pangs can be satisfied if she asks for a drink of milk, especially if she has learned the conventions of polite speech and prefaces her demands with 'Please'. Writing is a further step along in this process, whereby inner thoughts can be made into tangible written syllables for others to act upon. With assistance from supportive people in the environment, the child acquires a stock of appropriate mediators (words) and with practice soon develops fluency and control over language.

The zone of proximal development

This zone is defined by Vygotsky as the difference between what a child can do on his or her own and what can be achieved with assistance from someone who is more skilled. Assistance takes the form of 'demonstration, leading questions, and by introducing the initial elements of the task's solution' (Vygotsky, cited by Moll, 1990).

Vygotsky states that as a result of this assistance, 'what the child can do today with assistance, she will be able to do by herself tomorrow' (cited by Moll, 1990, p. 97).

Vygotsky's formulation of the zone of proximal development is of immense importance for children's growth, but it needs to be refined and developed further.

Tharp and Gallimore (1988) have developed a helpful four-stage model describing progress through Vygotsky's zone of proximal development, and concentrating on the change from where learning is regulated by others to where it is self-controlled. During **stage 1** the learner is given a model and guidance, but does not conceptualise the goal of the activity in the same way that the skilled assister does. Callum may imitate his mother's example with help, but he does not see that the letter he is writing should contain a specific message from him. He carries out the task alongside his mother who was herself writing a letter to Kim.

During **stage 1** there is a decline over time in the amount of responsibility taken by the assister and an increase in the responsibility accepted by the child. There is less give-and-take, and more independent action. During early writing, the child is confronted by a complex task, because of a daunting range of variables – from message clarity to spelling and letter formation – which has to be attended to, and his attention span is still limited. Much help is needed.

Stage 2 sees regulation pass from the assister to the child. As the child writes, she may say 'Here's how to make an *a*, now how do I spell *birthday*?' Vygotsky called this form of talk 'private speech'. Indeed, it is a commonly observed characteristic of anybody learning a new task. For example, an adult learning to use a word processor may constantly comment to himself about using the mouse to block lines and then finding the correct key combination to move a block of text. The learner is becoming autonomous. She sets her goals and provides her own 'scaffolding'.

Stage 3 is reached when the task is automatic and no assistance is required from others; nor is inner commentary necessary. The learning has reached a mature stage. Finally, in **stage 4** the competencies previously acquired may have decayed, and are no longer capable of accomplishing the task. The learner then goes back through stages 1 and 2. For example, a seven-year-old may draw a picture of an aeroplane in the middle of a story instead of writing, because he has forgotten how to spell the word 'aeroplane'. Drawing represents an earlier attempt to write and may here serve as a reminder to ask someone for the correct spelling later so that the drawing can be replaced by a word.

These stages should not be seen as all-encompassing or consistent. For some aspects of writing (e.g. use of capitals), a young child may be working through the early stages of the zone of proximal development; for other aspects of writing (e.g. handwriting) he may be at the third stage.

Co-construction as an explanation

Now we can build on the Vygotskian theories which explain how the individual child constructs her concepts about writing to arrive at a more detailed model of how society contributes to the process. The key assumption of co-construction is that children's own mental constructions and society's influence are constantly interacting. They are dependent on each other – hence the label 'co-construction.' Again, by *society* we mean not only the children's own families but also the wider communities in which they live. McNaughton (1995) has developed a series of propositions which describe the theory of co-constructionism, of how the growing child is socialised into literacy as she constructs her own mental world. The propositions are summarised and briefly discussed below, but for a fuller discussion the reader is referred to McNaughton's innovative book *Patterns of Emergent Literacy* (1995).

The first proposition is that **'families arrange time and provide resources which socialise children into their practices of literacy'**. In other words, children learn about literacy because story-book reading forms part of the regular family routines of the children described in this chapter. Trips to the library are frequent and there is a large number of children's books in each house. As well as books, writing paper and a variety of things to write with (pencils, felt-tip pens, crayons, chalks) were given to the children. Both our families sent their children to preschool for part of each day where there were books and materials for writing freely available to the children. Sometimes writing activities are done with the child, sometimes he observes and mimics. All these practices and experiences provide opportunities for children to construct personal images about the nature and functions of literacy. Families which fail to find time and resources to do this, start a cycle of disadvantage for their children which often continues through the school years.

McNaughton's second proposition is that **'family literacy practices**

reflect and build social and cultural identities'. Children acquire important cultural messages from their early interactions, messages which are built into their growing concepts about literacy and about their place in the world. Many families provide models of newspaper reading, others may spend more time with television. Some families provide environments where religious reading, singing and prayer are common; Samoan parents in New Zealand provide many models of long-distance letter-writing; some families serve on committees where the writing of minutes and notices are regularly observed; some provide excellent models for the homework habit; others have fewer functions for literacy in their daily lives. Contrasting cultural experiences in relation to emergent literacy are clearly seen in the widely quoted research of Heath (1983) in the United States and McNaughton (1994) in New Zealand. In the case of Callum, making Christmas lists is clearly favoured in his family. For other children, Christmas may have little significance, compared with other important cultural festivals. Hannah's mother commented that their writing was always done in the context of play and included writing letters to each other via a postbox, writing menus, reports of activities and diaries of visits.

The third proposition is that **'literacy practices are expressed in specific activities, such as goals, rules, and ways of carrying out the activity'**. In some families, mother chooses and reads the story right through, and only at bedtime; father may be more democratic and let the child choose or he may alter the story impulsively. In some families, the older sibling is expected to read or share the reading with the young child. Ninio and Bruner (1978) showed how some parents have a routine for getting children to label objects during picture-book reading sessions. Wells (1986) shows how some parents create in-depth discussions from their story reading. Literacy activities may be seen as a reward or a chore, as a pleasure or an experience to be endured. They may be set as a form of tutorial instruction, or to amuse, or to occupy time. The shape these practices take within a family strongly influences the construction that the child puts on them. Books may contain joys to be shared, or they are a bore. Writing can be a fantasy trip or a meaningless exercise.

Caregivers develop systems for the child's learning and development within the activities they perform – sometimes by themselves, sometimes with significant others in joint activities.

The preschool teacher, encouraging Callum to write his own name on his artwork, may provide a model, help him trace letters and break the word into segments. At other times, he has the C or double 'll' drawn to his attention in a street sign or a supermarket. Callum will sometimes practise writing his name by himself, as this is seen as an important skill which his caregivers do all the time. At other times, he will be guided, with models, with attempted constructions on his part, and with feedback and further models by adult helpers. The mental constructions which correspond to his physical attempts are gradually refined, soon to approximate closely his adult models.

The fourth proposition is that **'two basic and complementary types of learning systems occur, and each can be expressed in a number of ways'**.

One basic system is the tutorial system which gives the emergent writer guidance and assistance. All three children described in this chapter have a supportive tutorial system provided by the family and by the preschool they attend. The caregivers provide models, set joint activities, suggest structures, help them with the 'hard bits' and comment on performance. In Bruner's terms, they provide 'scaffolding' to help them through the early stages.

The other system is the personal system that children develop when they attempt to write by themselves. So a line of *Hs* for Hannah is an example of her personal system refining what she has already learned through assistance provided by her mother. Both learning systems are needed if the child is to benefit from supportive adults. Learners need the help of others and the opportunity to operate on their own.

Hannah's parachute

Proposition five states that '**what children learn to do with written language is become experts within particular activities**'. Some become proficient at labelling objects, some at recognising letters, some at learning prayers, some at retelling stories in their own words. What they do often is what they learn and become expert in. Such expertise is often not recognised or readily transmitted into another setting. So the child who learns the alphabet through singing the Sesame Street alphabet song, fails to reproduce this knowledge when tested in a different context from that in which the original learning took place.

The final proposition is '**development is enhanced by the degree to which settings are well co-ordinated in terms of practices, activities, and systems of learning and development**'. Children who are encouraged to write, with good models and appropriate tutorial systems, will move quickly into inventive spelling, where they construct their own attempts and learn to link symbols with sounds – a useful form of expertise for both reading and writing. At its simplest, this means that writing development will be quickest when there is communication between home, school and preschool and where parents and teachers share ideas about teaching and respect individual, social and cultural differences. It is essential, in the co-construction model, that preschool and school teachers build on the constructions that the child has already made about literacy, rather than reject it all and ask the child to start again. Expertise developed at home in letter production or name writing or reciting or labelling or book concepts can be the springboard to helping children move easily into the school's programmes.

 ## Transition to school

To amplify his theory, McNaughton (1996) and his colleagues have provided one of the few large-scale studies of children's writing that begins in the six months before they start school and continues during the first six months of their school career. Eighteen families drawn from three ethnic groups (Pakeha, Maori and Samoan) with a total of 19 children participated in the study. Using a range of techniques (interviews, observations, diaries, recordings by parents, anecdotal comments) the research team set out to describe the quantity and range of preschoolers' writing and coordinated this with a study of how the family literary practices and beliefs influenced the children's writing.

All children in the study produced a considerable amount of writing. This was in spite of the fact that some of the writing children produced was not available to the research team, because it had been lost or 'put somewhere' (p. 15). There were considerable cultural and economic differences among the families in the study but all children engaged in writing. In fact, the differences between families of similar economic and cultural status was as great as that between cultural and economic groupings. This was despite differences in child-rearing practices and beliefs about what it is appropriate for families to teach their young children. This finding is of value because it questions, for New Zealand, the popular belief that only children from white, middle-class families have significant literacy experiences at home before they begin school.

The researchers classified the children's writing into six categories.

Table 2 (McNaughton, 1996) shows the categories, together with the average number of pieces of writing collected across all subjects.

Table 2 – Writing categories and quantities from 18 families

Main writing category	Mean number of examples
Labelling	11.9
Naming	4.4
Narrative	10.3
Exposition and Argument	6.0
Messages	2.8
Diverse	3.8
Total	44.2

The most common category was labelling, of which the chief activity was putting names on drawings. Narrative was the second most common and then documenting events of significance in the family. Exposition and argument was a category which was much more prominent in home-based literacy activities than at school and often consisted of explanations for games, diagrams of models of cars, building plans for houses and directions for tracing genealogy. However, it is clear that narrative is not the only genre used in these early years.

In the month before school (when the children were aged 4 years and 11 months) the researchers saw a definite change take place in the children's writing. All of them wrote more, and there was a shift in emphasis from the rest of the family towards what were perceived as literacy activities appropriate for school. Thus, there was more emphasis on writing letters of the alphabet, especially when writing names. The mechanics of writing such as word spacing, alignment and the placement of words on lined paper, were stressed.

This study is important because it goes beyond anecdotal evidence from parents (valuable though that is) and systematically studies a group of diverse children using a range of techniques.

 ## Summary

We have accumulated a considerable amount of evidence which shows that writing occurs within the home environment and is an integral part of the lives of most families who construct a model of writing with their children based on their family traditions. The value of these early literacy practices finds theoretical support in the writings of Vygotsky, and more recently in the detailed observations and theorising of McNaughton. Unfortunately, the extent, and unique nature, of many family literacy practices has not been sufficiently recognised by teachers who have not been aware of the extent of writing carried out in the home, or of its significance to school-based learning. The meanings for literacy that they have constructed in their preschool activities loom large in their initial reactions to teachers' requests.

CHAPTER 4 Beginning school

'Progress as a writer depends to a considerable extent on increasing familiarity with forms of the written language … through reading and being read to.'
J. Britton, (1983) Shaping at the Point of Utterance

Beginning school is a time of enormous change in children's lives. They leave behind the security of friends, familiar preschool teachers and small groups of children to enter an awesome world of large numbers of children and unfamiliar teachers; a world where the day is marked out by bells and signals and assemblies and school rules. Even the toilets are no longer uni-sex, but marked 'Boys' or 'Girls'. Yet most children eagerly anticipate going to school and make the transition smoothly. Perhaps it marks another important step along the road to being grown up. Almost any child when asked to describe the difference between school and preschool will reply that 'at school you learn to read'. Writing does not appear high on the child's list of priorities of school-related tasks.

There may be an abrupt change in the life of the child, but the development of the child's writing skill need not be discontinuous at the point of school entry if teachers can discover and build on what the child already knows. As we saw in chapter 3, writing emerges early for most children. They scribble, they learn letters, they copy others and they learn about print concepts.

The age of school entry is socially determined. Children are neither more nor less ready to read and write at age five in New Zealand than at six in the United States or seven in Sweden. An implicit theme of this book is that writing is a learned skill, which is acquired in a variety of settings, and in a variety of ways, and not dependent on some in-built form of maturation from within the child. We do not carry within us a mental clock which rings when we have reached an age where learning to write suddenly becomes possible. So at age five the task facing the New Zealand child is similar to that facing a six-year-old American or a seven-year-old Swedish child – how to adapt to and flourish in a formal education setting.

Home/school differences

A major difference between school and home is the lack of common background between child and teacher. In the course of his major longitudinal study of children's linguistic development in England, Wells (1986) studied language interactions at home and at school. In many respects he found the classroom lacking in the features of 'an environment that fosters language development' (p. 87). At school, for instance, children speak less than half as much to adults, they express fewer ideas, and use less complex language. They rarely initiate conversations in the classroom, they ask fewer questions, and when they speak they more often use fragments, rather than sentences. Extending a child's meaning is considered a helpful way of enhancing a child's development. But in England it happens only half as often at school as in a typical home.

Wells quotes other British studies which confirm the results of his own. For example, 'at home, conversations were more frequent, longer and more equally balanced between adult and child' (Tizard and Hughes, 1984). There is clearly more that teachers could do to promote language growth.

One area where teachers are more active is in asking questions. Some of these are ones where the answers are known by the teacher and they can be confusing to children used to genuine requests for information. Other questions are prompted by a lack of shared experience between teacher and child. This is particularly so when writing is undertaken. Questions at home are genuine requests for information rather than the 'guess-what-I-am-thinking' questions usually asked by teachers. In the child case studies already discussed, the children only need to make the briefest of intentions known when they are writing and the adult is immediately aware of the context of the writing. Callum's mother knows only too well that he has been asking for a 'sonic game' for several weeks because his friend has one.

Because the parents usually know what has happened, they can interpret intentions, add detail, suggest modifications, offer correction where necessary. They are part of an ongoing shared narrative. By contrast, the teacher does not know the context of the story and has to elicit details by question and answer. Suddenly the talkative preschooler is reduced to one-liners – 'This is my house' or 'We went to grandma's place'. At school, a change takes place in the nature of the interaction between the child and the adult who does not have access to a rich fund of shared memories.

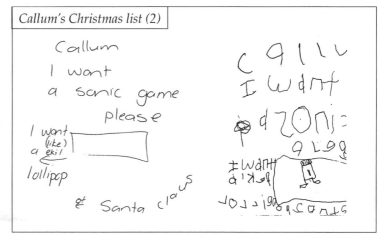

Callum's Christmas list (2)

The amount of time parents have available to spend with their children also decreases, but more importantly, there may be changes in the nature of the interaction. Before they started school, children's writing could be done alongside a parent who was preparing a shopping list or writing a letter; now any writing at home is confined to the time between coming home from school and going to bed. This is usually a busy time for parents who are often tired themselves and occupied with household chores. Often the child is tired from the day at school. So going to school brings in its wake changes in parent-child weekday interactions, changes which may not always be beneficial.

A further difference is that compared with school, a wider range of writing is done at home. In a study of 108 grade 1 and 2 children, Shook, Marrion and Ollila (1989) found that children wrote on a wider range of topics at home than at school. The children preferred to write about animals or people and used the format of notes and lists. Perhaps we should not be surprised with this finding when we remember the shared background that parent and child have in common. Children can draw on their network of family acquaintances for writing activities – both as recipients of writing and as subjects to be written about.

Characteristics of school learning

A variety of instructional techniques are deployed at school. However, compared with home or preschool, school learning is more structured. School is identified by children as a place where the serious business of learning happens. Formal instruction in correct letter formation may occur each day, as well as brief sentences dictated to the teacher which the child may be expected to trace over or to copy underneath. 'Correctness' becomes an imperative of equal importance to the child's message in writing a story. Just as there is a right way to sit on the mat at school (sit up straight) and a right way to answer questions (put up your hand), so there is a right way to write your stories with the right letter formation and the right spelling and even with the right sort of pencil sharpened to a correct point.

The case study children described earlier certainly had differing school experiences. The parents observed changes in their children's writing following school entry. For instance, Callum regressed from letter-like formations to scribble. What was distressing to his mother was the teacher's annotation 'Well done!'. His mother considered that, in comparison with his work before school, it was not at all well done. Rather than improving on his efforts to form letters that were closer in appearance to adult letters he had regressed to a form of scribble, which received the teacher's approval.

In Hannah's case, her first teacher was particularly gifted and Hannah's mastery of writing progressed rapidly building appropriately on her pre-school competence. But, after a successful first year, her mother noticed that her progress in writing apparently reached a plateau. Perhaps the novelty of school had worn off and the change from writing at home which was related to play or home activities that were spontaneous and not timetabled, caused a decline in Hannah's enthusiasm for the tasks. She did comment to her mother at this stage that writing was not as much fun because 'we have to have our feet flat on the floor and our bottoms on a chair, and I like being on my tummy to write'. Such inhibitions, however essential in crowded classrooms, do have their unanticipated effects.

Children's progress in writing depends very much on their progress in reading – and being read to. The processes are intertwined. We cannot escape the feeling that the school beginner has a great deal to learn, but in contrast to those unstructured preschool years, this new learning has structures, content and values attached to it, over which the young child has little control. The arbitrary nature of some of these rules and conventions make their learning even more difficult. School can be a bewildering place.

Reading is an important source of things to write about. Here is Hannah's letter written to Cinderella when Hannah was 5 years and 3 months old.

The letter reads 'To Cinderella I think you need to get out of your place your sisters are awful I love you love Hannah'. This was followed by a row of hugs and kisses. The letter was written at Hannah's grandmother's suggestion after she had read 'Cinderella' to Hannah. Hannah did not ask for any help at all. This sample shows that Hannah can use writing to empathise with Cinderella, to express her emotions and to offer advice. These understandings probably contribute more to Hannah's development as a writer than her considerable grasp of the mechanics of writing – shape, directionality and spelling.

Hannah's letter to Cinderella

 ## School entry knowledge

Most teachers would like to build on what children bring to school. So, many attempts are made to identify what they know or can do when they arrive at school. These attempts are not always successful, as some pupils are reluctant to demonstrate their knowledge to strangers. Nevertheless, some general findings are of interest.

Children entering school in New Zealand at age five can identify 14 or 15 letters and write two words, one of which is usually their name. In reporting this statistic McNaughton (1995) comments that there is a wide range of variation in this figure. A British study (Tizard and Hughes, 1984) showed that a quarter of five-year-olds studied could write their own names.

McNaughton suggests that rather than look for explanations of varying achievement at school entry in sweeping generalisations invoking ethnicity or socio-economic status, we should examine differing family practices within social and ethnic groups. As we saw in Chapter 3, they contribute much to children's writing development. A further complicating factor is the narrow range of ways schools assess their new entrants' knowledge which may not reflect the full range of writing activities the child can practise.

Shook, Marrion and Ollila (1989) found that the first and second grade Canadian children they studied had well-developed concepts about the nature and purposes of writing and that 94% of their sample classified writing as an enjoyable activity they perform at home while just 57% preferred to write at home rather than at school. The researchers comment that perhaps at home the children were free from 'requirements such as spelling, neatness and [correct] grammatical usage' (p. 137).

School instructional practices

Beginning writing practices in schools vary widely depending on the philosophy and experience of the teachers and school policies. Clay (1987) describes three possible approaches, all different, to writing instruction for the child beginning school. In the first approach, children are systematically taught letter names and shapes by means of workbooks and systematic teaching. Clay comments that the principle is not one of discovery but of somehow impressing the form of the word on the child by having him sound it, read it, and write it many times. This is strangely different from what the preschooler does naturally in discovering writing (p. 52).

The second approach, popularised by Ashton-Warner (1963), has the child draw a picture and dictate a caption to the teacher. The child then traces over the writing or copies it underneath. Over time there is a shift from the teacher providing the bulk of the writing to the child doing more and more unassisted. This approach, referred to as the Language Experience Approach, is consistent with a Vygotskian approach to writing where the teacher provides assistance to the child in their zone of proximal development but gradually transfers responsibility to the child. It also has the added advantage of starting with the child's own thoughts and feelings. With appropriate actions by the teacher, the child will retain enough ownership to feel pride in the writing and will want to read it to others.

A third approach is to let the children write without any attempt to impose a model of either letter formation or spelling on their work. The form of the message is invented by the child as it is transferred to the paper. Over a period of time, and especially as progress is made in learning to read, the messages grow to be more like adult writing with conventional printing and spelling. This method is the beginning of the process writing approach described in later chapters.

Clay (1987) argues that each method has its strengths and disadvantages. Most children will learn to write eventually, regardless of the methods used in school, but the important question to ask is whether the method establishes the child as someone who enjoys writing. Heenan (1986) cautions against the formal systematic approach that Clay refers to in her first statement. He argues that by using models which children imitate they are being constrained with notions that there is only one way to write.

> *'In the first days at school, children develop a dependence on the teacher, absorb the attitude that writing is difficult – impossible without supervision, and limited by the whims and dictates of the class teacher. Children are soon conditioned to play it safe, sacrificing spontaneity, freshness and independence for correctness, teacher approval and dependency.'*
> *(Heenan, p. 10)*

We would suggest that, using enjoyment and fluency as criteria, the last two of Clay's methods would be best for beginning writers.

An analysis of the writing of the three children used as examples in this chapter, suggests that Hannah's teacher would be the most successful in achieving these goals. Langley (1994) interviewed Hannah's teacher to discuss the factors she considered important in explaining Hannah's successful mastery of the process. It was clear that the teacher had recognised that Hannah began school already knowing a lot about writing. Within the class the teacher was accustomed to using a shared approach to writing, whereby the children worked collaboratively to produce a piece of text. The teacher had clear objectives for the writing sessions, the most important of which was 'getting the message down, getting the story down without it being a big deal' (p. 15) The teacher accepted the children's unconventional attempts at letter formation and letter-sound relationships. A lot of the teacher's time was spent supporting the children by 'just going round and telling them how well they have done... and in letting them share with the rest of the class' (p. 15). Her letter to Jenny shows how well this has been achieved.

Hannah's letter to Jenny

After two-and-a-half months at school, Hannah already knows she can write. Her letter reads 'Dear Jenny, I can write and now I am five I know lots of things, Love Hannah'. This letter was written unaided and her spellings for 'Dear' 'write', 'five' and 'know' were all close approximations.

Each child in this class has an individual list of objectives for writing and these are crossed off as they are attained. Hannah's teacher also reported that while her children usually write about themselves, they also write 'true stories' and non-fiction. The different genre the children chose to write in were influenced by what they were reading at the time.

The success of this teacher's programme can be attributed to both the universal characteristics of good teaching and the specific characteristics of her literacy teaching. Enthusiasm on the part of the teacher, and children experiencing success in what they are doing, underlies all good teaching whether it be in maths, science or music. Specific, achievable objectives are related to literacy. Links with learning to read are made obvious and the children's attention is drawn to similarities and differences between learning to read and to write. Notably absent from this teacher's practice is any whole-class instruction on the mechanics of writing – letter formation, spelling and grammatical structures. While these aspects are not ignored in individual cases of need, they are secondary to the main focus of the writing which is to convey meaning. Hannah is not seen as an empty vessel to be filled with knowledge about writing. Hannah's teacher fosters links between home and school by inviting parents into her classroom before the children begin school and subsequently by explaining her teaching methods to the children so the parents can participate as much as they choose in fostering their child's development at home.

An example of the effectiveness of the programme is shown below. Hannah's story reads 'I am very sad because my friend died. It was Gilly. And Grandma is very sad because he died. Hannah'. Gilly was an old dog who belonged to her grandmother. Hannah's mother explained that when Hannah visited her grandmother she told her mother not to say anything about Gilly's death. A week later she wrote about the death at school.

This is a remarkable piece of writing not only because of its technical skills (correct letter and word formation together with punctuation) but also because it shows that a young child has learned about the power of writing to record momentous events – events that are for Hannah, more easily written about than spoken. The story is carefully structured with an

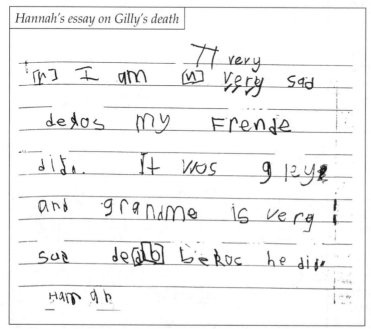

Hannah's essay on Gilly's death

opening sentence, an elaboration and a comment, to make a coherent statement about an important event in her life. She already knows that writing can be a powerful tool in helping her understand the complexities of the world – and that knowledge lays the foundations for a mastery of this way of communicating. That she chose to write this message at school also reflects the caring nature of the classroom and her teacher who has established an atmosphere where the children feel safe, not only to attempt to write original messages but also to express their emotions.

The success of these methods contrasts markedly with traditional approaches to the teaching of writing, which are outlined in the next chapter.

Writing development in the early school years

Kroll (1991) studied a class of American children for five years, beginning with their entry to school. Four children were selected from the class and their work studied in detail. Kroll identified four strands in the development of writing which became apparent from the study of this class – **physical**, **semantic**, **symbolic** and **social**. The most fully developed strand Kroll identified is the semantic one which can be further subdivided into

1   the relationship between drawing and writing

2   differentiation of literary genres such as narrative, exposition and poetry

3   coherence within text

4   the influence of heard and read literature on structure, style and content

5   the manifestation of part/whole coordination within the writing domain.

Each subdivision has the potential to be described developmentally. For example, if we consider stages **2** and **5**, Kroll identifies the beginnings of differentiation between genres at year 1 when writing showed the beginnings of a narrative structure. Year 2 writing was dominated by narrative, with stories having a beginning, middle and an end, although Kroll notes that the narratives lacked development, or trailed off at the end (p. 11). By year 3, the children's writing consisted mostly of personal narrative with signs of experimenting with narrative fiction. There was also experimentation with some expository forms as well. Scott (one of Kroll's subjects) wrote commercials and recipes as well as narratives. Year 4 saw the children writing well-structured narratives with the 'overall impression of a well-formed story' (p. 15). There was also more experimentation with different kinds of narrative and the beginnings of expository prose. By year 5, 'Narratives, descriptions, personal narratives, expositions all have definite characteristics that the children make use of' (p. 19).

Kroll's study is valuable because it describes the development of a group of children over a period of five years, during which time they were taught by a number of different teachers each with a slightly different classroom emphasis. However, all of the teachers encouraged a variety of writing – stories, journals, reports. It would appear that differences in orientation or emphasis among teachers may not adversely affect children's writing providing the teachers hold similar underlying concepts about the process of learning to write.

We do consider that there is a danger that any stages can be seen as immutable and not susceptible to change. The conditions affecting learning (such as entry to school, teacher behaviour and peer interaction) all contribute to learning to write. While the product can, with hindsight, be analysed into stages, it would be a mistake to think that these stages are mutually exclusive and impervious to school and curriculum influence. We do not regard development (of almost any educational kind) as a series of inexorable stages the learner passes through. Rather, we see a dynamic interaction between the developing writer, the environment, and the school curriculum.

McNaughton et al. (1996) found the amount of writing done by his New Zealand sample varied depending upon the school. The six families from McNaughton's study described in Chapter 3, went to three different schools. In two of the schools, the children produced, in six months, double the number of pieces of writing that they had generated in the six months preceding school. Children attending the third school, however, produced less than they had in the six months immediately before attending school. These findings have to be interpreted with some caution because, in the controlled environment of the school, it is easier to collect systematically and keep children's writing. In addition, in the school where the children wrote less, the teacher withdrew from the study after two months. Although the children wrote more at school, their range of writing was more restricted. For instance, no child wrote messages at school – an activity that was prominent in all pre-schoolers' writing. Naming, narrating and describing were the most common kinds of writing.

In an attempt to bridge the gap between home and school, McNaughton et al. (1996) conducted two experiments with the teachers of the children studied from between age 4:6 and 5:6. In the first experiment, a portfolio of children's work, done at home before beginning school, was assembled and shown to the teachers. Although the teachers were interested in the portfolios and looked through them carefully, little change was seen in their interactions with the children. The second intervention saw each child take home a booklet in which he/she was to draw and write with the help of the family. The next day at school, the children would talk about, and show to the teacher the things they had drawn and written about at home. Through analysing teacher/child interactions, the researchers showed that this intervention was effective in building links between the culture of the home and of the school.

In another case study of ten four-year-old New Zealand children, Berwick-Emms (1989) investigated how typical ways of interacting with family members in the home helped or hindered their progress at school once they turned five. She observed the children in their home environments at regular intervals, and then again once they started at their various primary schools. It was clear from the results that the teachers' expectations of behaviour fitted much more closely with the typical behaviour of some children than with that of others. Indeed, the number and variety of school instruction patterns observed in the home correlated more highly with success in reading and writing activities at age six than did the children's measured ability at age five. Some parents, for instance, organised their children's day, encouraged them in reading and writing, read to them often, directed their television viewing, played games with their children, asked questions which required thoughtful answers, and took a genuine interest in their talk – expanding and elaborating in such a way as to assist their language development.

Such 'behaviour codes' were absent or rare in other homes, and the children from such homes were found to be at a distinct disadvantage once they started school. They were unable to work out the point of their classroom activities, to cope with distractions, or to concentrate on the tasks in hand.

While Berwick-Emms's sample was small, the individual case studies revealed vividly how the mismatch between home and school behaviour codes can be a major cause of failure in children's early literary experiences.

Many changes which occur when the child begins school are not discussed in any systematic fashion in the research literature. We can only speculate on the effect they may have on children.

Summary

Starting school is a major milestone in a child's intellectual development. In some respects, schools provide fewer opportunities for children to develop oral language. But the diversity of reading resources, the encouragement to write regularly, and the presence of a trained teacher, do assist their written language growth.

Of Clay's (1987) three major approaches to introducing children to writing at school, we believe the language experience and process writing, using children's invented spelling, are more effective in a child-centred curriculum. Teachers need to find out what children can do in writing and build on their early strengths.

Kroll's longitudinal study (1991) of American children showed systematic phases in children's writing and a real diversity of genres in the early years. McNaughton et al. (1996) found that appropriate home interventions can help build links between home and school. Berwick-Emms' study (1989) revealed something of the mis-match that occurs for some children between home and school routines, and the consequent disadvantages for such children.

5

Traditional approaches to writing: focus on the product

'Large numbers of children enter school as eager learners and writers, and leave it as reluctant writers.'

H. Hood, (1995) in R Ward (Ed.) Readings about Writing

Rapid changes in educational methods are unusual in education. Nevertheless the last ten years have witnessed a veritable revolution in the way teachers in many western countries have viewed the development of children's writing. This chapter outlines and evaluates the assumptions and methods of the traditional approaches to teaching writing in the primary school; traditional approaches in which writing development meant focusing on the product, rather than on the process.

Writing has traditionally been viewed as a simple educational skill. It was a skill that pupils had to learn by studying the products of good writers, by practising each of the various subskills, (spelling, grammar and punctuation) and by having their efforts assessed regularly in relation to the teacher's expectations about what was clear, correct writing. It was widely assumed that children would gradually improve if they:

1 wrote regularly on topics assigned by the teacher

2 prepared a plan before writing

3 worked in relative silence to produce their writing

4 wrote for the teacher as audience

5 ensured that spelling and grammar were correct

6 handed in all their work for correction by the teacher

7 studied their mistakes in order to avoid them next time.

As for the teachers, it was assumed that they should:

1 provide children with models of good writing

2 instruct the children in grammar and punctuation

3 have the class study class spelling lists

4 mark with red pen the errors in children's writing.

At the same time, what little research there was on children's writing focused on such issues as the best way to grade children's work, the optimal frequency of writing, changes in the length of sentences and numbers of subordinate clauses produced with age, and the influence on writing of teaching about formal grammar and spelling.

Thus, traditional approaches focused on the *product* rather than the process. Children were shown what to aim at, and how far they had approached the ideal, but they were given only minimal assistance along the way.

Unfortunately, the traditional approach to writing was too rarely successful. Some children learned to write creatively and confidently, in spite of the methods used, but surveys of student attitudes to writing, and surveys of the amount of writing that children did out of school, or after they left school, only confirmed the impressions of many teachers that school writing lessons were unpleasant and unprofitable for the majority.

For instance, in 1945 and again in 1955, Ford (1955) surveyed the attitudes of children in 22 Canterbury (New Zealand) classrooms towards their various subjects. In the case of boys, the results were clear. In 1945, out of nine school subjects, writing was ranked 9th in popularity by boys aged 9, 10, 11 and 12, and 8th by 13-year-olds. Girls in each age group from 9 to 12 years ranked it 7th. Ten years later, in a similar survey, the pattern was almost identical. Clearly, writing was not popular then.

In 1984, a similar survey was conducted by Elley (1985) on a cross-section of 75 Canterbury classrooms. Boys typically ranked writing 6th out of 7 subjects, just ahead of music or social studies. Girls ranked writing 4th out of 7 subjects. The popularity of writing was still not high enough to suggest that teachers had found a way to make it a pleasurable school subject for most children.

Regrettably, the picture was little different in other western countries. In the US, the National Assessment of Educational Progress (NAEP, 1990), found attitudes to writing generally to be negative. For instance, in 1984 the percentage of Grade 8 students who 'like to write' was only 38.9%; the percentage of Grade 4 students who agreed with the statement 'If I didn't have to write for school, I wouldn't write anything' was 33.4%. American students showed little enthusiasm for writing in the early 1980s. Furthermore, achievement levels showed no improvement from 1974 (NAEP, 1990).

The picture in Great Britain was no better. In a national survey of attitudes to writing conducted amongst 11-year-olds in England in 1982 (Gorman et al., 1988), 38% agreed with the statement that 'they only write when they have to' and 40% 'look forward to the time when I won't have much writing to do'. These findings are consistent with inspectors' reports in 1979 which noted 'the tedium of much written work in schools'. The typical pattern in British schools was 'one of notes and essays, interspersed with the practice of answering examination questions, alongside drills, exercises and tests' (quoted by Gorman et al., 1988, p. 175).

Likewise, in a study of writing instruction in eight schools in Scotland (Spencer, 1983) children were found to write very little extended prose. Most agreed that writing was the 'hardest' aspect of language, and 36% said they preferred to copy notes from the teacher rather than write their own ideas on paper.

Studies of traditional writing instruction

Many studies of classroom routines have confirmed the generally negative picture presented above on the main features of traditional writing. In New Zealand, for instance, Philips (1985) made an intensive observation study of the writing activities undertaken by children in two intermediate school classes (years 7 and 8) and two high school classes (years 9 and 10) over a period of five weeks. Amongst other findings, Philips showed that:

1   Most writing was brief, routine and factual, rather than extensive or creative. Extended essays represented 15% of children's time in years 7 and 8, but less than 5% in years 9 and 10.

2   Many children preferred to spend more time on preparing to write, on layout, drawing, doodling on their page and other avoidance tactics than on writing.

3   Pupils rarely revised or edited anything they wrote.

4   Most pupils showed little enthusiasm for writing.

In a larger study of Year 8 and Year 11 students in New Zealand, conducted by the International Association for the Evaluation of Educational Achievement (IEA) in 1984, Lamb (1987) showed that, in writing lessons:

1   Students were usually allocated a topic to write about at both grade levels.

2   Students usually wrote for a teacher, and the teacher typically provided feedback in the form of written comments rather than grades or marks.

3   Class discussion was typically used to promote ideas but most writing was individual.

4   Girls showed greater competence in writing than boys on every criteria and on every type of writing task.

5   Only 10% of Year 8 and 8% of Year 11 students rated themselves as 'good' at writing.

6   Analyses of spelling errors in 1984 showed very similar accuracy rates to those shown in a large-scale survey by Nicholson in 1970 (Lamb, 1987).

7   Thirty-seven percent of Year 11 students agreed that 'Most of my friends dislike writing'. Only 22% disagreed.

8   In a writing task which required students to give advice to a friend on how to do well in writing in their school, the most common responses referred to surface features such as presentation, correct spelling and punctuation. Such a response was out of line with teachers' professed emphases, which were starting to change in New Zealand at that time. It may reflect the attitudes of parents and other adults, or the fact that such aspects are easier for pupils and teachers to identify and describe.

While there were some encouraging findings in this IEA survey, it was clear that, in pupils' eyes, there was a lack of vitality in many of the schools' writing programmes. In her summary of student responses, Lamb commented that:

> *'these responses describe a picture of classroom writing as copying other people's writing, without any apparent development of their own skills in narration, description, analysis or argument, or much practice in writing for a range of purposes and audiences... the most frequently addressed audience is the teacher.'*
> *(Lamb, 1987, p. 159)*

Research in other countries which participated in the IEA writing survey of 1984 showed similar patterns of student response and teacher practice. They differed in one respect, namely in that teachers in other countries tended to put more emphasis on formal instruction in grammar, a feature which had steadily declined in New Zealand (see Chapter 11).

Research on the assessment of children's growth in writing was also outcome-based. Hunt (1965) and Loban (1976), for instance, described pupils' writing development in terms of syntactic maturity, and showed pupil growth in terms of changes in sentence length and T-units (main clause and its dependent phrases or clauses). Aspects such as growth in awareness of audience or drafting patterns or sense of organisation were rarely studied. Harpin (1976) showed how children's finished writing changed through primary school, on such measures as word count, sentence length, clause length, index of subordination and personal pronoun indices. Such measures showed very slow improvement with age, with much overlap between phases, but gave few leads as to how the growing process might be speeded up.

Carlin (1985) developed these indices further, and showed that while the averages did show gradual increases they were unhelpful for interpreting or guiding the progress of individual pupils. They were insensitive to gender differences, and concealed real growth in other key dimensions.

Applebee (1981) drew attention to a striking contrast between the traditional 'product' approach and more recent process approaches in an analysis of teachers' attitudes to children's errors in writing. Table 3 (adapted from Kroll and Schafer, 1977) reveals how the two different philosophies affect both the questions researchers ask and the strategies that teachers adopt. In the product approach, students are 'passive recipients of the accepted wisdom'. Errors are annoying, to be avoided or stamped out. In the process orientation, the student is assigned a constructive role, as a learner who is actively developing hypotheses about the nature of language, and testing them out in his/her writing. Errors are expected, and exploited for what they reveal about the student's current hypotheses.

Table 3 – Contrasts in teachers' attitudes to writing*

	Product Orientation	Process Orientation
Why study errors?	To produce a taxonomy of the errors learners make.	To produce an explanation of why a learner makes an error.
What is the attitude towards errors?	Errors are 'bad' and to be avoided.	Errors are 'good' for what they reveal about the the learner's hypotheses.
What shall we do about errors?	Attack and eliminate them through drill and overlearning.	Understand the source of errors and the rules that give rise to them.
What can we discover about errors?	The source of failure in the student and/or the programme.	The strategies which lead the learner into error.
How can we account for error?	Error is a failure to learn the correct form.	Errors are natural. They arise from learners' active strategies, overgeneralising, incomplete rule applications, etc.
What are the goals of instruction?	Eliminate errors by establishing correct, automatic habits.	Assist the learner to approximate standard forms; support active learning strategies; be tolerant of errors.

*Adapted from Kroll & Schafer (1977)

Conclusion

It is clear that the traditional emphasis on the products of children's writing generated few constructive pointers on how teachers might assist their pupils' development and produce fluent writers who liked to write. Not until researchers started to focus on how good writers actually operate and began to understand the processes young children went through, and experimented with new ways of motivating them and guiding them as they worked through these processes, was real progress made.

The largely negative picture presented in this chapter can be overdrawn. There were some pupils who emerged from school enthusiastic about writing and New Zealand has recently been noted for the vitality of its children's authors. Some teachers and/or parents have been doing something right in individual cases. Nevertheless, on a broad scale, the traditional approach stands indicted on the grounds that too many pupils disliked writing and indulged in it all too rarely. If they never wrote they would not be expected to improve. The time was ripe for a new approach, the process revolution, which emerged during the early 1980s.

Graves and the process approach

*'The teaching of writing demands the control of two crafts – teaching and writing.
They can neither be avoided, nor separated'*
D. Graves, (1983) Writing: Teachers and Children at Work

This chapter describes the theory that views writing essentially as a process, rather than a product, and then considers the research evidence and logical arguments which support this theory.

More than any other person, Donald Graves (1983) has shaped the way we teach writing in schools today. Indeed, the term 'process writing' is almost synonymous with the work of Donald Graves. It was he who opened classrooms in the United States and elsewhere to fresh ways of helping children write. His insights spawned a wave of research and reform in the eighties and nineties. The genesis of Graves' thinking lies in the dissatisfaction he felt at the lack of progress American children made when taught to write by the traditional approaches of the sixties and seventies (see Chapter 5). His work, widely accepted in New Zealand, Australia, Canada, and North America, is the basis for the practical ideas set out in the New Zealand Ministry of Education publication, *Dancing with the Pen* (1992). Indeed, process writing has become part of a unified approach to language teaching, including reading, and fits under the all-purpose general label of whole language teaching. A clearly articulated pedagogy supports the Graves' approach to learning to write.

What is process writing?

The rationale for all of Graves' work has its origins in the opening sentence of his 1983 book. 'Children want to write' (p. 3). They are natural writers, keen to express themselves. Yet in Chapter 5 we described how writing is among the least popular of the school subjects. How can this be?

Graves argues that schools have traditionally placed obstacles in the way of children writing and too often ignored the knowledge about writing that children possess when they begin school. Schools had made writing unnecessarily difficult for children to learn. This had to be changed.

Graves' philosophy and the pedagogical methods which have grown out of it are breathtakingly simple. No specialist equipment is needed – no textbooks or workbooks or exercises. The children decide what to write, they write every day, they talk about it with others, they revise and produce multiple drafts of their work, and finally they present it in some form for others to read. The only essential requirement is the presence of teachers who understand the philosophical principles which underpin process writing, who see their role as primarily recognising the children as writers who are to be supported and guided as they work on their writing. The teacher follows the lead of the children and offers advice and assistance as it is required by the children.

Two key concepts of process writing are **control** and **ownership** of writing. If children are to continue to 'want to write' they must be in control of the process. They must decide on the topic, and the way in which it will be approached. In this way, the child develops a sense of ownership, a sense of 'I am the authority here'. Process writing requires that the child write often, every day. The child's writing goes through a series of drafts. There are conferences with the teacher, it will be shared with peers, and finally, it may be published in some form.

As in the whole language approach to reading, meaning is central to the process. The child's focus should be on conveying meaning. Grammar, spelling, handwriting, layout are seen only as means to the end of conveying the meanings to intended readers, never as ends in themselves. A daily writing period is considered essential in the classroom because, just as whole language advocates consider that reading is learned by reading, so writing is learned by writing, not by exercises in grammar, spelling, handwriting or copying model essays. Children must practise their craft, daily, at a predictable time, under predictable conditions. The term 'workshop' is used in the United States to specify a time of day when children and their teacher, develop and practise the craft of writing.

Key concepts

1 Ownership

Because each child has chosen what to write about, it is his/her own topic and one to which each one is committed. This is in contrast to traditional writing classrooms where the class is assigned topics to write about by the teacher, or topics are drawn from a theme the class is studying. Usually the topic has been decided upon by the teacher, or the dictates of a national curriculum (see Chapter 5). Such decisions remove ownership from the child and place it in the hands of the teacher. Graves recommends that children choose their own topic, at least 80% of the time in the early years.

2 Drafts and revision

Writing is seen as something that evolves. It does not spring onto the paper in a pure, finished version. Rather, it is like a piece of clay which needs to be pummelled and smoothed constantly, with additions here and removals there, until the writer is satisfied with the final product. Successive drafts should clarify meaning, correct spelling and grammar, and produce a readable product. Along the way advice should be sought from peers and the teacher. While writing is popularly construed as a solitary activity, the process of writing successive drafts and the changes that are made usually need input from a variety of people. What happens during conferences with others can be explained by reference to Vygotsky's theory. The children receive and then internalise the feedback from their social environment to further their understanding of how to write for a real audience.

3 Conferencing

The conference is where most teaching takes place. Here, pupil and teacher meet and discuss the writing done. The teacher serves as audience and editor, asking a series of predictable questions which allow the pupil to explain what he/she is trying to say, how he/she feels about it, and where the problems are. Again, the child is the authority. The teacher should not take over. Most conferences will focus on a single aspect of the writing. If the child needs help, for instance with dialogue, then that is enough. The teacher does not discuss the spelling problems, the handwriting or the layout and the organisation at first. Usually, the first conference for a piece of writing will focus on getting clarity or organising; later ones on surface features, in preparation for publishing.

An important purpose of the conference is to show learner-writers how an audience reacts to their writing, where they are assuming too much and need to provide more detail, or where they are being repetitive, or getting off the track. If this is done often, pupils soon learn to put themselves in the shoes of their audience/readers. This skill is a key stage in the process of becoming a writer, a stage which was neglected in the traditional teaching of writing.

Some conferences are scheduled and intensive; others are roving, over-the-shoulder affairs, to encourage and show continuing interest. Sometimes the conference is conducted by a group, with or without teacher guidance. The conferences should always be 'tailor-made', constructive and helpful, and avoid negative judgements.

4 Publishing

If children are to invest themselves deeply in a writing task, it should have a real purpose. Usually the purpose is to convey information or to recount a story for other people to read. However, if it is published, it takes on greater importance for the child. Others will see it. It will be shared. Personal diaries and self-expressive writing are exceptions to the public nature of the finished product, but generally young writers should write for an audience. Again, they should decide which of the many forms publishing will take. For instance, it could be a wall story; it could be a letter to a sick classmate; it could be word-processed and put into a book for the rest of the class to read, or it could be filed away in the writer's personal file.

Thus, 'publishing' is a broad term with many different faces. Graves considers that publishing is important 'for all children. It is not the privilege of the classroom elite' (p. 55).

5   *Teacher modelling of writing*

Graves (1983) considers it to be of prime importance that the teacher should write with the children. Teacher writing has multiple effects on the children. Primarily, they begin to see writing as an activity which everyone does. It is thus removed from the category of so many school activities which send a message to children of 'do as I say rather than do as I do'. The teacher is creating a powerful model for writing if the children see her writing with them.

Graves suggests that teachers use a variety of techniques to model the process (writing on large sheets of paper, writing on overhead transparencies) and that they verbalise their actions so children can not only see the product of the writing but also hear the thinking processes which accompany the writing. By writing themselves, teachers will not only be providing a model for the children, but also helping them gain insights into the difficulties and delights of writing. They will be transforming the classroom into an environment sympathetic to writing, one where everybody participates equally.

 ## Implications for teachers

These underlying concepts of process writing required most teachers to change their beliefs and actions about teaching language. They had to see themselves as participants with the children in an ongoing process. Timetables had to be adjusted to allow for daily writing. The teacher role changed from that of an authoritarian figure who allocates topics and assesses the finished product, to one of assisting, guiding and encouraging the children. The role is not to dominate and dictate what should happen in writing time. These changes require a teacher who is confident in her own understanding of how writing is best fostered, who knows how to guide and assist her children, and above all, who is prepared to relinquish a large measure of control of the process to her children. She must be prepared to live with ambiguity and accept that writing on any topic can have acceptable multiple outcomes.

To implement Graves' work fully requires more than just setting in place a series of steps for the children to follow within the classroom. It is possible to set up a process of daily writing, conferencing and publishing and yet not have a classroom that embodies the ideals of process writing. In a successful programme, all children are seen as having something of value to write; all children, given the proper environment, will want to write, and above all else, the teacher must relinquish direct control. Instead of teaching skills to her preset agenda, she must be prepared to follow and guide the children in the directions they choose to take their writing. The teacher must act as a mentor rather than the font of all knowledge about writing. To use a term which seems now out of fashion in this era of accountability, the classroom must be 'child-centred' rather than 'teacher-dominated.'

How successful is process writing?

Implementing a process writing approach means that the teacher must adopt all aspects of the model, rather than only a few. This holistic feature makes it difficult to evaluate in any all-encompassing formal evaluation. Nevertheless, critics and parents will want to know that the teacher and the schools are fulfilling one of their key roles and fostering their children's literacy. Is teacher assertion sufficient evidence of success? Parents may be convinced by a portfolio of written work that their own child is making acceptable progress towards literacy. But how many portfolios do policy makers, evaluators and politicians have to see to convince them that this is an appropriate way for an entire school system to teach writing?

Proponents of a process approach to writing tend to use anecdotal evidence to support their claims about the efficacy of the method. They argue that one-off formal essay tests on assigned topics are incompatible with a process approach, because they are narrow and unlifelike. Objective measures of children's writing, such as word counts, also have their problems. Are longer stories of better quality than shorter stories? Should spelling, punctuation and grammatical correctness be the guides to quality? The problems of assessing the efficacy of a process approach to writing mirror the problems of assessment in writing generally and are discussed in Chapter 15. Many proponents of the process approach (Graves, Calkins, Hood) work collaboratively with classroom teachers and describe the results of their work in anecdote and story. Indeed, we depend mainly upon the intuitions of good teachers for our understanding of the benefits of process writing. Qualitative data is the norm and quantitative data the exception. One difficulty is that the writing of Graves and Calkins reports only the success stories. In the end, everybody produces worthwhile work. Are there no failures with process writing?

A fair evaluation of a process approach to writing requires the reader (whether teacher, parent, researcher, administrator or politician) to look at its results through a qualitative lens and not rely only on quantitative data in the form of numbers and tables. Nevertheless, we must avoid confusing observations with outcomes. What appears to work well in some classrooms may not be so productive in others. If process writing is so effective, we should be able to detect its benefits in more and better writing, and in more enthusiastic writers in many classrooms.

Evidence for the efficacy of the approach will be discussed therefore under the broad headings of: overall philosophy, comparative classroom research, and an analysis of the components of the process.

The philosophy behind process writing

Graves' concepts have their counterpart in the work of Vygotsky (1962). He recognised that learning is a social process, dependent on everything in the surrounding environment. By centring writing in the classroom, which above all else is a social place where children and adults meet, talk, and undertake shared activities, Graves is also acknowledging the social context for writing. This context in turn leads children to write about the things that are important to them in their social life – parents, siblings, friends, television, holidays and the like. Vygotsky's theory that learning first occurs in the social setting and is then internalised is supported by evidence from an examination of the content of children's writing. What the child has discovered from the external world has been transformed in his/her internal world and is expressed in writing. To use Vygotsky's terms, there has been a shift from interpsychological functioning (between people) to intrapsychological (within an individual mind) functioning.

The emphasis placed on conferencing, in Graves' position, particularly conferencing with the teacher, is supported by Vygotsky's notion of the zone of proximal development, which refers to the difference between what people can achieve by themselves and what they can achieve with assistance from a more skilled person. The assistance provided by the skilled person is represented by the concept of scaffolding which was developed by Bruner, one of Vygotsky's interpreters. Scaffolding provides an intellectual framework, a facilitating context, which allows a task to be completed. Then the scaffolding is gradually removed and the learner copes on his/her own. In Graves' approach, judicious questioning and commenting about a piece of writing provide the scaffolding for the writer's ideas to be further developed and clarified. The writer is then better able to develop and clarify without the same level of support. Thus, some of Graves' key concepts and practices can be derived from the writings of one of the twentieth century's greatest psychologists.

To be more specific, however, we can question Graves' contention that children are writers in the same way that adults are authors. Adults may write for a variety of audiences in a variety of ways. They do not always write fiction. Their working habits vary widely – they may write continuously for hours, or in small creative bursts. They may write in solitude or in a team, with rich resources around them or in a barren attic. They have considerably more control over their working environment than do children. Pupils are required by law to attend a school which functions within a clearly prescribed timetable. They must write when they are told to, rather than when the spirit moves them. The classroom has a limited space for working in – usually a choice of ill-fitting desks, group tables, or sprawling on the floor. The audience for an adult piece of writing – whether newspaper article or novel – seldom has direct access to the author. When children's work is published in the classroom the author is present and able to answer questions and defend or praise the work. Stories are the dominant classroom genre but most adult writing is more functional.

Thus, it is clearly an exaggeration to claim that the writing environment in a classroom can operate in the same ways as in the adult world. But the intention behind the analogy with adult writing is commendable. Teachers can do much to bring the two writing contexts closer together.

Personal narrative appears to be the dominant form of writing in a process approach. Young children naturally prefer it. They like to write stories, real or imaginary. Other genre are largely ignored. An emphasis on personal narrative can lead children to over-value the personal aspects of writing and neglect its important instrumental functions (see chapter 8). We suspect that different kinds of writing require different pedagogies. We cannot leave all writing to personal choice and still fulfil the requirements of the curriculum. Stotsky (1995) for instance, considers that a process approach leads to an excessive emphasis on personal narratives, to the detriment of other genres. She goes on to suggest that informational writing, requiring a different structure from that of personal narrative, may be neglected in schools. Empirical evidence for the value of personal writing as an aid to learning is lacking, according to Stotsky (p. 766).

Social theorists (e.g. Lensmire (1994)), argue that Graves pays insufficient attention to the role that class, race and gender play in inhibiting children's writing and that the process puts too much emphasis on writing as a purely individual process. Delpit (1988) is one such critic. She argues that process writing, with its emphasis on children's 'voice' and authenticity may disadvantage American black children, who need to learn to write in language which is acceptable to the mainstream. Many blacks have not had the helpful preschool experiences with books and writing that their suburban counterparts have. To catch up, they need specific instruction in mainstream writing skills. It is true that much of the research supporting process writing is conducted with white middle-class students by middle-class teachers and the results cannot be generalised to an entire population.

Delpit expresses her criticisms of process writing as follows:

> 'Progressive white teachers seem to say to their black students "Let me help you find your voice. I promise not to criticise one note as you search for your own song." But the black teachers say "I've heard your song loud and clear. Now, I want to teach you to harmonise with the rest of the world".'
> (Delpit, 1988, p. 18)

She argues strongly against an interpretation of Graves' work that sees fluency valued above all else. While Delpit wants more structures and 'rules' of writing taught systematically, she is not arguing for a wholesale return to traditional ways of teaching writing.

Perhaps she is fighting against an extreme interpretation of process writing. Purposeful writing is one of the tenets of whole language – and the language code used must be determined by the purpose of the writing and the audience. In some cases of personal writing, dialectal variations are entirely appropriate; in other cases standard English is the appropriate form. Nothing in the writings of process writing advocates precludes teachers from modelling these distinctions for their children and expecting them to follow suit. Delpit raises questions as to whether 'progressive' teaching methods can compensate for deprived early childhood literacy experiences by enriching children with more opportunities to read, talk, write and be read to. We suggest that children from all cultures learn incidentally and are capable of making choices – provided they are given the opportunities. South Pacific children, for instance, who are raised in an oral culture, when given an enriched reading programme at school do learn the conventions of writing in the same way as children from more literate traditions (see Elley, 1991).

There is a criticism that Graves' recommended strategy focuses too much on promoting children's individual voice. Some critics see it as solitary, individual, unsociable. However, we have used Vygotsky's theory to suggest that the genesis of children's writing lies outside themselves, in their social interactions, which are based in their cultural/historical settings. Moreover, when we take into account the conferencing procedures that multiple drafts of the writing go through, and the class discussion of pupils' efforts, we see that even the surface aspects of writing are not usually the product of just solitary work.

Other critics have argued that the numbers of children in each class make a process writing classroom difficult to manage. Walmsley and Adams (1993) surveyed 71 teachers in upstate New York about their experiences implementing process writing. The teachers' concerns ranged from feelings of personal inadequacy, to lack of resources, to limited time, to problems with state-wide assessment techniques. Many New Zealand teachers too, have complained of insufficient time to hold conferences with each class member. Resourceful teachers have found ways of scheduling their time to ensure that every child gets some conferencing time with the teacher each week, on a daily rostered basis, and more time working with peers in group conferences.

Hood (1995) has concerns that process writing has been introduced piecemeal to a school, and that children are confused by differing expectations that teachers have of their writing as they change teachers. When discussing the New Zealand Ministry of Education official view of writing, Hood says:

'We believed that writing was too important a life skill to allow teachers to follow a variety of opinions and interpretations. We felt that each school needed to develop a sense of vision... that all would be expected to follow. We believed that only then would we see a general improvement in the standard of written language teaching.'
(Hood, 1995, p. 5)

Process writing, if it is to be successful, he says, must be adopted on a school-wide basis and not left as a matter of choice for individual teachers.

The issues outlined above need resolution within the school if an effective policy is to be agreed upon. Children do need the security of a consistent policy, but there is surely room for some diversity of approach when writing for different purposes. Graves himself allows for 20% of writing time to be devoted to 'directed' writing.

Comparative classroom studies

One traditional approach to evaluating a strategy like process writing is to design experiments, and compare classes of pupils taught by different methods. So far, few studies have been conducted comparing the results of a number of classes who have a traditional writing programme at school with classes that follow a process writing approach. This may be, in part, because of the difficulties of matching classes who are identical in every respect except in the way in which they are taught writing. Also, the belief of many whole language practitioners that traditional methods of assessing writing are too restricted, may be another factor contributing to the lack of valid comparative studies. Eventually however, writing produces a product, which is read by a reader who passes judgement on what has been read. So one of the factors in evaluating a process writing approach must be some form of analysis of the product. If process writing is a successful strategy, then pupils who practise it often should become better writers – in due course.

In his extensive, widely quoted review of writing research, Hillocks (1986) was able to locate very few studies which compared process writing with more traditional approaches and was therefore unable to draw any conclusion about its effectiveness. However, one early study which has often been cited is that conducted by Linda Clarke in Toronto in 1985. She followed up a class of six-year-olds for one year, and compared them with a control group taught by a more traditional approach. The process writers' class chose their own topics and were encouraged to use invented spelling. Overall, she found that they wrote sooner, wrote more, used a wider range of vocabulary, but also made more spelling errors in their writing. (Clarke, 1988). Perhaps this latter finding is not surprising, as the process writers were being more adventurous in their choice of words, and were getting less help. However, it is significant that by the end of the year, the process writers did perform significantly better on a standard spelling test of 50 words. A supporter of Graves would no doubt claim that they were beginning to take responsibility for their own spelling progress, because they saw the need for it.

Clarke's study was encouraging, but was too small to be definitive. Moreover, it appears that the children in the process writing class were taught reading using an explicit phonics approach, which may have affected their spelling development and biased the findings (Stahl et al., 1996).

New Zealand research

One large-scale New Zealand study was conducted by Swarbrick (1989) who compared five classes of Year 4 children who had been taught using a process writing approach (for a period of four years), with six comparable classes which had been taught with a more traditional skills-based pedagogy. The variables she compared were spelling skills, writing quality, range of vocabulary used, and attitudes towards writing.

The results of her study showed that there was little difference between the two groups on every variable on a set writing task. The process classes tended to make slightly more spelling errors in their writing, and to like writing less, but on all other variables neither of the groups was superior to the other. Swarbrick cautioned that her results may have been contaminated because she could not guarantee that her control group had not been exposed to elements of process writing during their time at school. Teachers often work in an eclectic way and it is difficult to find examples where a particular pedagogy is adopted in a 'pure' form.

There is also the worrying problem that a single writing task, assigned by the teacher, however interesting it might be, is not a realistic enough task for those taught by process writing methods – especially when the assessment is made on the first draft.

Swarbrick made the interesting comment that perhaps 'it takes the enthusiasm of a Donald Graves to make this procedure work more effectively than the written language teaching procedures which were being used by the teachers of the control group classes' (p. 24). Our reading of the literature on process writing suggests there is indeed a high degree of personal commitment by the teachers and researchers who work and publish in this area. Is this personal zeal sufficient evidence to support the almost universal acclaim process writing receives from its practitioners? It is possible that Swarbrick's cross-section of teachers lacked some of these qualities. Hood's surveys (1994), for instance, suggest that many teachers do not implement process writing well. But the study should give us pause for thought.

Another, more encouraging New Zealand experimental study, which focused on the way in which teachers respond during conferences to the writing of five- and six-year-olds is instructive. A.M. Breen-Williams (1992) compared the effects of a 'message-oriented' conference style to one in which the teacher focused only on surface features. Working with first- and second-year children in four classes, for seven months, two teachers deliberately responded only to the content or message of the children's writing during conferences, while two other teachers of comparable groups, responded only to the children's spelling, punctuation and handwriting. The children wrote every day and chose their own topics to write about.

Writing samples were collected by the researcher at regular intervals and subjected to both quantitative and qualitative analysis. Tape recordings were also made of samples of the teacher-child conferences to check on the strategies used.

Although the time period of the study (seven months) was relatively short, some clear trends did emerge. The six-year-old message-oriented group used a significantly wider range of vocabulary in their writing, suggesting greater confidence in their ability to express themselves. The five-year-old message-oriented group showed significantly greater clarity in their writing, and produced greater impact on their readers. Perhaps the most encouraging finding was that there were no differences in the progress made by both groups in spelling, punctuation and other surface features even though the message-oriented teachers gave little attention to these. Their pupils were apparently taking responsibility for learning such matters themselves. In this study, then, teachers who responded to their children's message, and not to their children's mistakes, appeared to help their children more.

Another positive New Zealand study is the one reported on in Chapter 9 by Jerram et al., (1985). Here, a Graves-type approach led to large gains in quantity, quality, spelling and vocabulary of nine- to ten-year-olds in an Auckland primary school.

American comparative studies

In an American study, Varble (1990) compared matched pairs of Grade 2 classes and Grade 6 classes where one group had been taught writing by traditional methods and the other had been taught by process writing and whole language methods. The researcher went to great lengths to ensure minimal overlap in the teaching practices of the contrast groups. Three raters, who did not know to which group the children belonged, assessed their writing both for quality of content and for mechanics (spelling, grammatical correctness, punctuation). The raters were given carefully specified criteria by which to assess the work and inter-rater reliability was high. The results showed that second grade children in the process writing group scored higher on content than children taught by traditional methods. The results were statistically significant. Just as in the Breen-Williams study, there was no difference for the mechanical aspects of writing for grade two. At the grade six level, however, there were no differences in content or mechanical aspects for either group.

This was a carefully controlled study using 248 children and three independent raters. That the second graders did much better than their traditionally taught peers on the quality of content is of interest; what is even more interesting is that their traditionally taught peers did no better in the mechanics of writing, defined as words spelled correctly, correct punctuation, complete sentences, correct grammar and usage (p. 247) than did the whole language students who did not receive class-based direct instruction in these skills. As whole language advocates consistently claim, the mechanics of writing, when taught in isolation, do not easily transfer across into the complex task of writing a story.

The sixth grade results were puzzling. Perhaps it is difficult to find children who during their entire six school years have not been exposed to a mixture of teaching styles. Eclecticism rules in most schools. Also, the fact that children were taught by process writing methods only in Grade 6 may not be enough to offset the habits and attitudes of the previous five years.

In a longitudinal study, Manning et al. (1990) followed a smaller group of children for three years, from kindergarten to the end of second grade. Twenty-two inner city children were divided into a whole language group and a skills-based approach group. At the end of the three-year study, the whole language group were found to view themselves as better writers and they outperformed the skills group on measures of spelling achievement.

In another study comparing whole language instruction with skills-based teaching using two second-grade classrooms, Monteith (1991) found that children taught in a whole language classroom obtained higher writing scores on the Stanford Achievement test in writing and had more positive attitudes towards writing.

Thus, the empirical research on process writing is encouraging, but not yet conclusive enough to stand alone. More work is needed.

 Evaluation of particular components

1 Topic choice

Graves (1983) considers that the child's choosing the topic is a foundation-stone for process writing. He writes (p. 21)

'The data show that writers who learn to choose topics well make the most significant growth in both information and skills at the point of the best topic. With best topic the child exercises strongest control, establishes ownership, and with ownership, pride in the piece.'

Note that the teacher is assigned a role in this development. Writers 'learn' to choose topics. This learning requires a thorough knowledge of each child, on the part of the teacher. According to Graves, it is promoted, too, when children help each other on topic selection. The Ministry of Education Handbook, *Dancing with the Pen*, for example, claims that when children choose topics for themselves, they retain ownership and have a purpose for their writing (p. 31). When translating these ideals into daily classroom life, however, practitioners are more equivocal. Free choice of topic, for instance, is not always available to children. When writing on a curriculum topic, such as a science field study, the choice is necessarily limited.

Moreover, children do not exist in a vacuum, and cliché'd rehashes of television soap operas often make up much of children's daily writing. Willinsky (1990) found that when given unfettered topic choice the boys he studied wrote 'violent story after violent story' while the girls wrote stories where 'princesses wake up, dance with princes all the night long' (p. 128). Graves (1983) devotes three pages to a teacher-child conference where the story is about weapons and destruction ('if you pull the pin on a grena [grenade] you hav to thw it quk or it will blooenup in yr had' (p. 128)), without any response to the cliché'd and bloodthirsty content. Not surprisingly then, teachers often discourage pupils from pursuing some topics, and many still insist on setting the topic at the outset. Only then can they ensure that all kinds of topics and genres are attempted.

2 Conferencing

In his 1983 book, Graves devotes considerable space to the place of conferencing in a process writing class. He is uncharacteristically prescriptive here, going as far as to diagram (p. 98) the seating arrangements between child and teacher for the conference. There should be a range of predictable questions asked during the conference which will:

open the conference

follow the writer's information

deal with basic structures

deal with process

reveal development.

This is a formidable list to work through and implies that conferencing is an on-going process over a period of time. Each conference should focus on no more than two or three outcomes.

Calkins (1986) feels that the teacher's primary role in a conference is to react to the content of the writing. She describes the teacher's role as to 'be a person' and 'to enjoy, to care and to respond' (p. 118).

Hood (1995) suggests that many of the conferences he has seen in schools are a 'waste of time' (p. 49) in that teachers use them to focus only on the surface features of the writing and do not explore the content.

Fitzgerald and Stamm (1992) studied the influence that group conferencing had on two Grade 1 children, abstracted from a larger study. They found that the conference affected each child's writing differently, depending on whether the child entered the conference with some knowledge of good revision activities but little practice in revising – in which case the conference was valuable – or whether the child entered the conference with both knowledge of and practice at revision – in which case the effect of group conferencing was minimal. These conferences involved children as well as the teacher. An important finding from this study is that similar conference procedures can have differing outcomes for individual children depending on their individual needs.

3   *Drafting and redrafting*

Multiple drafts of a piece of writing are a key feature in a process writing classroom. Drafting is a process whereby children gain further control over their work. Graves writes (p. 4):

> 'Many eight and nine year old children can do extensive revisions of a single selection, rewriting well over six to eight drafts to get information the way they want it. Children write this many drafts because they have taken control of the writing process. They are writing to find out what they mean themselves... Children revise because they want the information to be accurate, to make good choices about what they should say, what should be discarded.'

Drafting is not simply a matter of making a good copy after a 'rough' copy has been made. It is a way of clarifying ideas as well as attending to the surface features of the writing. Graves (1979) sees the process of revision in writing as no different from revision in other media such as drawing or playing with blocks.

There is a developmental sequence observable in the ability to make successive drafts. In the case of beginning writers little or no revision is done. Once they start, they tend to focus first on spelling and handwriting.

Eight-year-olds find it easier to revise topics about personal experiences than about the experiences of others. Gradually, they begin to add, delete and reorder content, but all these stages overlap one another. Some will start to insert interesting descriptive words, and replace bland or hackneyed ones. The ideal is that 'children begin to internalize revision and conference themselves when they are not being conferenced' (Heenan, 1986, p. 75). Graves describes this sequencing pattern based on anecdotal evidence gathered during his study of pupils in a school in New Hampshire.

There is, however, a danger in imposing a strict ages-and-stages view of drafting and revising. Obviously as children master the basic technical skills of handwriting, spelling and grammar, the focus of their revisions will shift towards content and away from surface features. That appears to be the trend. But it does not preclude young children from changing their marks on a page to make them 'say something else' nor an eight-year-old changing the content of a report about her class visit to a nearby farm. Indeed, good teaching requires continued encouragement to do just that. Descriptions of what is common in children does not imply prescription of what they should do.

Calkins sounds a note of caution about drafting when she writes:

'We need to guard against an attachment to revision for revision's sake. There is nothing inherently good about making additions to a text nor is there anything inherently good about revision.'
(Calkins, 1986, p. 136)

Fitzgerald (1988) however, sees a clear need for drafting and revision. She suggests three guidelines for successful revision:

1 It should be one part of a complete writing classroom which is designed to foster good writing.

2 It should focus on the process and not the product.

3 It should be seen as a way of thinking where the teacher, as well as the children, constantly revise their thinking.

4   A practical concern

Lensmire (1994) carried out a year-long study in a Grade 3 classroom during writing workshop time. He used a combination of field-notes, teacher and classroom documents, audio tapes, student interviews and student writing as a way of studying writing workshops. While he found much that was valuable in a workshop approach, where everyone in the classroom wrote on self-chosen topics at a set time each day, based on the Graves philosophy, particularly in the playfulness and enjoyment students experienced, he also expressed concerns about some of the end uses of the children's writing. He described the experiences of Jessie (p. 384), an unpopular child with her peers. Jessie became the butt of scorn in stories written by other children as in this example (p. 385):

> *'When we got into the classroom on Monday morning we heard singing. It was Jil, Jessie and Paul. They were singing a dumb song that went like this: "Let's get together, ya, ya, ya". Mrs Parker was out of the classroom. Then Lisa shot Jessie in the back. AAAAAH! Jessie said with a scream!'*

Oral abuse ('Zit face') was used in children's writing and directed at Jessie. Lensmire claims that the social, economic and gender divisions of the community outside the classroom were also present and reproduced in children's writing during workshop time. Lensmire writes that

> *'The writings of workshop advocates are replete with romantic portrayals of innocent, straightforward children pursuing individual writing projects within the workshop. Such portrayals help workshop advocates ignore serious problems and issues that attend workshop commitments to student self-expression and control – for example, the problem of children pursuing questionable intentions and material in their text, such as when a violent, sexist story (with thinly veiled attacks on a female classmate) represents the "authentic voice" of a group of boys during sharing time'.*
> (Lensmire, 1994, p. 389)

Lensmire, while supportive of many of the goals of a process approach to writing, sounds a note of caution. His comments are valid. The reduction, or even the abolition of a teacher's authority, together with the child's control of the choice of topic and ownership of the writing may not produce writing which is suitable for the classroom either in tone or content.

Similar experiences are reported by Dudley-Marling (1995, p. 255):

> *'Today Paul wrote a letter to Nader. I was pleased because Nader is often excluded by other boys. But when I saw the note later it read: "Nader, I'm going to beat you up after school".'*

Summary

Graves' ideas have had a profound influence on the writing programmes of many teachers. His methodology is derived from an analysis of the way adults write, adapted for the classroom. Children choose what to write, and how to write it. They are the authorities. They tell others how it goes. Anecdotal evidence is used to support claims for the efficacy of Graves's methods. His methods encourage teachers to place an emphasis on enlightened classroom practices rather than to focus on each individual's cognitive structures. Indeed, Graves' work (which has been the basis for a 'school' of writing research – see the work of Cambourne, Chapter 7) sees its best exemplars in child-centred, progressive school systems.

However, it is naive to expect that a freeing up of the conditions under which children write in classrooms is sufficient to break social barriers and herald a new age of understanding between children. Extravagant claims for the benefits of a process approach to writing have often undermined its many virtues. Nor must the adaptation of a process writing approach result in a *laissez-faire* attitude on the part of the teacher where all content is equally acceptable. Classrooms are social places. They must be observed at multiple levels. Attitudes held by the class members towards gender, race and class will be reflected in the children's writing. Some of the implicit rules that classes are governed by are not necessarily those which teachers would wish to see codified in children's writing.

It is possible that in their enthusiasm to create a child-centred, progressive classroom, scholars such as Lensmire have downplayed the role that teachers play in the process-oriented classroom. Our reading of Graves' work suggests a powerful role for the teacher, particularly in conferencing and decisions about publishing. Graves' latest writings emphasise that the teacher is not merely a spectator in the classroom, but has an active role to play in all aspects of the writing process (Graves, 1994).

There is a need for further empirical and qualitative study of process writing, but it should be informed by a proper understanding of Graves' position. Process writing, without an active teaching and conferencing role for the teacher, is unlikely to produce competent, enthusiastic writers.

Cambourne's model of literacy learning the natural way

'Learning to become literate should be as uncomplicated and barrier-free as possible.'

B. Cambourne, (1988) The Whole Story

This chapter outlines Brian Cambourne's popular model of how children can learn to write naturally and builds on the process model of Donald Graves. Cambourne is an Australian teacher-researcher, who has worked at Woollongong University since 1982. His views are derived from many hours of research and observation 'in classrooms, homes, backyards and supermarkets'. His teaching methods are widely known and adopted in many classrooms in Australia, New Zealand and North America.

As a young teacher, Cambourne was puzzled about the inability of many of his pupils to learn literacy, even though they were readily capable of many other complex tasks – like competitive sports or card games or learning their own oral language. These pupils had no deficits when it came to

> *'mastering the skills, tactics and knowledge of complex sports like cricket, or sight reading music or running a successful lawn-mowing business, or understanding the racing guide, or calculating odds associated with card games, or translating across two or three languages.'*
> (Cambourne, 1995, p. 183)

So why couldn't they learn to write in school?

The answer he arrived at, after 20 years of observation in classrooms, was that the prevailing pedagogy of Australian teachers was at fault. Most teachers followed a learning theory that assumed that learning literacy was largely a teacher-controlled process of building correct habits through regular practice and extinguishing 'bad connections'. For such teachers repetitive drill and practice of optimally-sequenced sets of habits was the key to efficient learning. Such a theory of learning was contradicted by his observational strategies of toddlers learning to talk. The success of this 'stunning intellectual achievement' seemed to follow quite different rules.

Eventually his field studies in many Australian classrooms led him to an alternative view of language learning which has acquired a respectable place in current thinking about literacy acquisition (Cambourne, 1988; 1995).

Conditions for language learning

Cambourne's observations of young children grappling with literacy tasks led him to the view that human evolution has given us a nervous system that learns language naturally and easily, given certain conditions. The diagram shows how eight basic conditions are required, that they are interrelated, that they are all dependent on the pupils' engagement, and that they are facilitated by four more classroom processes which produce good literacy learning.

1   *Immersion*

If children are to acquire oral language readily, they need to be immersed in it frequently. This is the natural state of affairs for most children, but not for deaf children or 'feral' children, who are isolated from human contact at an early age. Likewise, if children are to learn to write they must be surrounded by print, they must be read to, and they must have access to books and notices and posters and songs and poems and environmental print. They need ample access to good quality text.

Figure 1 *A model of classroom literacy learning (from Cambourne, 1988)*

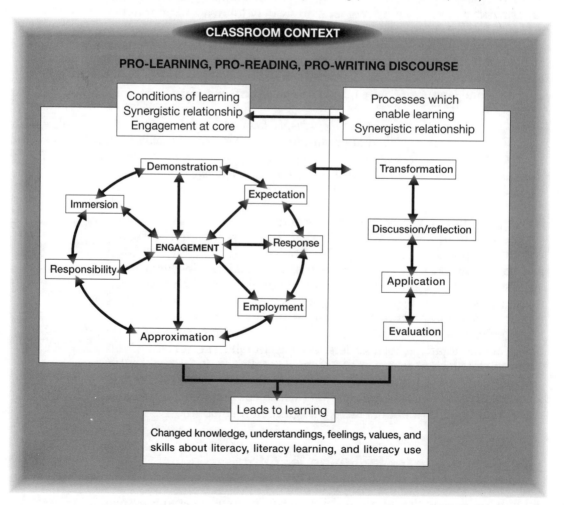

2   Demonstration

Preschoolers learning to talk have many models provided by parents, siblings, peer groups, television and radio. They are surrounded by chatter from an early age. It is not surprising, then, that they learn the language and styles of speech of their community. Likewise, children who are learning to write must see adults struggling with the same process. Shared writing is a key feature of Cambourne's model. When teachers compose a letter or report in front of their pupils, and talk aloud about their ideas and problems in doing this, the pupils learn much about the process, the structures, and the strategies that are needed. They learn much about the conventions of language in an ongoing authentic literacy task. Many such experiences are required in learning to write.

3   Engagement

Immersion and demonstration are required in learning to write but they are not enough. Children must also engage or participate actively in a language event if they are to learn from it. Learner-speakers become involved in many conversations. And learner-writers need the same kind of regular involvement if they are to benefit. They must see real point or purpose in their writing tasks. As Cambourne puts it, in an automotive analogy,

> 'the "clutch" of learning needs to be connected to the "power" of immersion and demonstration if there is going to be any "movement".'
> (1988, p. 51)

Why do some children fail to engage? Sometimes because they do not see themselves as potential 'doers' of the activity they have observed. It is not for them. Sometimes it is because they don't see a need for it. Or it's too hard, too risky. Their efforts will only result in criticism, or mistakes to correct, or even ridicule. Or perhaps they have too little respect or liking for the teacher. If teachers know their pupils, and are aware of these potential obstacles to engagement, they can plan to overcome them. Engagement is a central condition which is essential if other conditions are to 'click'.

4   Expectations

Parents expect their children to learn to talk and send strong messages that they are capable of doing it. Likewise, teachers and parents should provide similar messages that writing is important, that their children will learn to write, and that their progress in this process is valued. It means too, that the teacher should know her pupils well enough that the expectations will be realistic. A modest effort of two short sentences, unconventionally spelt, from one pupil may be cause for celebration, while much more might be expected from the child next door. Sometimes the expectations have a 'hard edge': 'We need to work on this more, Richard, before we can send it to the Mayor'.

5   Responsibility

Children should be free to choose what they will pay attention to in any language encounter. It is their responsibility to learn to talk and the models cannot be preprogrammed in the optimal sequence for them. Likewise, if the literacy learning situation is natural, rather than contrived, the child will again have the opportunity to take responsibility for deciding what to pay attention to. It cannot be programmed for him/her on the curriculum writer's assumptions about which language is simple and which is complex. This is a judgement for the learner to make. And taking responsibility for one's own learning is critical to learning something as complex as language. There is so much to learn that it cannot be left to a curriculum developer to package it in the right way for each child. The learner must be in control.

6   Employment

Children need frequent opportunities to employ their growing skills, whether talking or writing. They need to use language, in a variety of contexts, for real purposes, and to learn from the success of their communications. Learner-speakers are encouraged to practise – by naming objects, by retelling experiences, by role playing, by making up stories. Likewise, budding writers need to practise writing every day, sometimes for the teacher, or a family member, or the local council, or a friend in hospital, or a pen-pal or the class next door. For Cambourne, learning to write is a by-product of use, where the focus is on meaning and purpose, rather than on form. As children write they realise what they still need to find out and thus have incentives to find out.

Under the category of employment, he allows for the practice of language forms when talking or writing to oneself, as an audience. Young speakers often talk in seemingly nonsense words for themselves, in long monologues, and become more confident in their articulation. Young writers should also have the opportunity to play with language, without serious intent.

7   Approximation

Young writers will progress in language learning if they are prepared to 'have a go' and to risk making errors. However, sympathetic teachers/parents should not discourage this behaviour by voicing serious criticism of the faults. We don't expect babies to produce fully-formed sentences, or use adult grammar. We accept their approximations to pronunciation and to word sequencing as stepping-stones along the way. Indeed, studies of parent-child interactions show that most parents respond to the truth or meaning of their child's utterances, not to the immature grammar or faulty word order. Oral language learning proceeds under such conditions of tolerance. So literacy learning should encourage and accept approximations. The child will hypothesise, test, change the hypothesis and test again if the adult allows them the freedom to experiment. If error-free productions are expected, then production will quickly dry up.

8   Response

Children need feedback if their language is to grow and converge on adult patterns. They need a response to their 'employment' efforts, some 'significant other' to fill the gaps in their approximations, to react to their messages and to encourage further production. The teacher's response should be informative and non-threatening, and should focus on the message rather than the format. Often it will entail another demonstration, an alternative way of communicating the same message without penalising or condescension. Sometimes it will suggest a source of help, such as another child or a dictionary or a wall chart.

Classroom applications

Cambourne has spent many hours attempting to apply these eight conditions in classrooms, working with local teachers as co-researchers. One lesson they learned from these experiences was the crucial role of engagement. While the other factors might be present and helpful, if the student was not engaged then they were ineffective.

In addition, they identified four other practical classroom 'processes' which together acted with the eight conditions and facilitated the children's learning.

1   Transformation

Learners need to transform their learning until it is 'uniquely theirs'. They should feel that they own it. This may require rewording, or paraphrasing teacher models until the writing has a personal stamp on it.

2   Discussion/reflection

Social interaction with their pupils will often result in new interpretations, more mature meaning constructions, and more insight about how one's own language production is understood by others. Reflection, which is a kind of discussion with oneself, will often help learners to make explicit their knowledge about literacy, their awareness of how language works (metalinguistic awareness). Cambourne thus encourages lots of talk about books, about pupils' writing attempts, and the problems they face. The writing classroom can often be noisy.

3   Application

This process is implied by the **Employment** condition (above). Pupils need frequent opportunities to apply their developmental writing skills in a context where other pupils will discuss their common problems, and reflect on them. One can learn much from solving other students' writing problems.

4   Evaluation

Pupils are constantly evaluating their own efforts, no matter what skill they are practising. They should be encouraged to assess their own work, while teachers and peers are providing external feedback to check against their own.

How are written texts constructed?

For Cambourne, writing is inextricably bound up with reading. One cannot write well unless one has previously learned to read, and the writing process always entails some re-reading of what one has already constructed.

In explaining how we build our own texts, Cambourne distinguishes between subconscious and observable components.

1 Subconscious behaviour

In planning a piece of writing – whether a letter to the Minister of Education, or a shopping list – one begins with a subconscious intention to undertake a particular task. The precise details about its form will come later.

Cambourne's research showed that experienced writers then have to face up to several decisions – still largely subconscious. These involve such questions as the purpose of the writing (why?), the nature of the intended audience (for whom?), the information needed to write (what do I need?), the content (what about?) and the procedure (what first?).

Given good classroom conditions, learner-writers can also learn to plan their writing in this way. In traditional classes, they have too often been conditioned to focus on surface features, such as spelling and handwriting.

In Cambourne's terms, writers have available to them a 'linguistic data pool' or repertoire of knowledge about forms of words and ways of sequencing them which they can draw on to help make their decisions. They will know something too, about their topic and their potential audience. The way they select from their data pools will determine the shape and success of their writing. This process is still largely subconscious.

Thus, if the pupil is telling a story, he/she would call on the data pool for the general features of narrative (setting, characters, plot, complication, resolution, conclusion) and use such a framework – still unconsciously – to organise the writing. The data pool would also be called on to provide appropriate conventions, words, and categories of words – to allow suitable words for the setting (descriptive), words for events that happened (past tense verbs), dialogue (speech marks), language to entertain, and so on. By contrast, an expository passage, which provides information about an elephant, or a haunted house, or a new environmental policy, would require a different structure, and a different choice of words. While the topic will constrain the choice of words, to some extent, the writer's knowledge about the needs of the audience will also influence the choice of vocabulary – whether abstract and technical, or concrete and commonplace. To acquire the linguistic resources needed for these decisions, young writers need to engage with many examples of writing, to see others writing, and to see how different audiences respond. Of course, the decisions are not all made at once. The process is rarely linear, but tentative and progressive. Good writers change their first drafts and their intentions as they re-read them, reflect on them and talk about them.

Cambourne attaches much importance to the subconscious decisions. Indeed, he suggests that a good writing programme would help learners become consciously aware of the meta-textual processes that we go through in planning to write. Children need to understand how their early decisions about their purpose, and audience, and content can affect their writing; how writing is supported by reading and talking; how fiction text forms differ from non-fiction, from persuasive passages, from letters, lists, recipes, memos and other genres; and how good writers construct text. In view of Cambourne's emphasis on the eight classroom conditions for effective writing, he would not suggest that these meta-textual features be taught directly in the abstract, but that pupils would discover them in the course of their daily engagement with a variety of texts, with the aid of discussion, reflection and external response.

2   *Observable behaviour*

While writers are planning, subconsciously, they also carry out the overt behaviours which result from their planning. Cambourne's young writers would typically talk about their intentions and decisions, and then begin writing. This would be followed by reading of what was written, reflections on the earlier decisions. They may make immediate changes to intentions, or strategies, or words written, or they may consult a peer, or a book, for further ideas, and then write on, in a repetitive cycle of writing, reading, talking, reflecting and more writing. These phases are what others call 'pre-writing, writing and rewriting,' but he cautions against such a simple, straight-line image of the sequence of operations.

Summary

Cambourne's ideal writing classroom has much in common with that of Graves. Children write every day – though not at a set time – for a range of real purposes and audiences. They are immersed in print, they see many demonstrations of real writing, they talk about their own and others' writing, and how it works, they have a sympathetic audience to respond positively and constructively, and their writing is published or used for some genuine function. The classroom will often appear 'chaotic' (see Cambourne and Turbill, 1987), but it will be a cooperative one and the pupils will know what is expected. They will feel secure if they understand the point of the conditions and are prepared to take responsibility to learn the conventions, in due time, through their own engagement. And they know that their approximations will be accepted for what they are. Under such conditions, children will learn to write in a natural way, and come to enjoy writing in the process.

8 Cognitive psychological models of writing

'For children first learning to write, the mechanics of the process clearly take up most of their mental capacity, and they have little left over to devote to such concerns as content.'
    C. Bereiter and M. Scardamalia, (1982) From Conversation to Composition

Chapters 6 and 7 described a process approach to children's writing. One objective of a process approach is to mimic, as much as possible, the way in which professional adult writers write. This chapter draws on the work of cognitive psychology to reveal in greater depth how expert writers operate, and the developmental challenges that young writers have to face in moving towards mature writing.

 ## The model of Flower and Hayes

Cognitive psychologists study how we think – how we plan, make decisions, solve problems. Two cognitive psychologists, Flower and Hayes (1981; 1984) have described a powerful model of the psychological processes involved in writing. Their model describes how mature writers operate – from planning to translating and revision. It is derived from their research with adults explaining what they do as they write. A second model, that of Bereiter and Scardamalia is described in the second section of this chapter. They set out to describe how children typically attack the writing process, the underlying constraints they face, and how these constraints may be overcome in the classroom.

   The approach taken by these theorists is one which attempts to break down the writing process into component sub-processes. They assume that writers have limited capacity for attention. So trade-offs have to occur in the way in which they allocate attention to these sub-processes. Thus, the more attention the writers have to pay to memory, the less they have available for translating into words or for thinking about punctuation.

   Hayes and Flower (1980) describe their model as a cognitive process model which they contrast with a stage model. A stage model implies that writing can be broken into three discrete linear stages – planning, writing and revising. Planning occurs before writing, and writing occurs before revision. By contrast, their cognitive model takes the view that the processes involved in writing are 'recursive' and that the observable stages of writing (planning, writing and revising) can and do take place throughout the process. All these activities are intertwined. One plans, sets off writing, reconsiders the plan, writes more, revises the first section, plans further steps, revises the plan, and writes again.

Figure 2 reproduces the Flower and Hayes model. As can be seen here, the task environment, the writer's long-term memory and the writing processes constitute the major elements of writing in the Flower and Hayes model. These are represented as three separate boxes, linked by a series of arrows. *Task environment* means anything external to the writer – the writing task, the text as it is written so far, the teacher, and the classroom surroundings, as well as the child's own home. *Long-term memory* refers to the writer's information about the topic and how it is stored, as well as information about the audience for the writing and about the genre used. The third element, the actual process used, has three sub-processes – **planning**, **translating** and **reviewing**, all under the control of a **monitor**. All these elements have to compete for attention. So, the more familiar the topic, the less attention need be paid to it, and the more attention there is ready for the translating tasks such as ordering, word-choice, spelling, punctuation or paragraphing.

Figure 2 *Schematic model of expert writing proposed by Hayes and Flower (1980)*

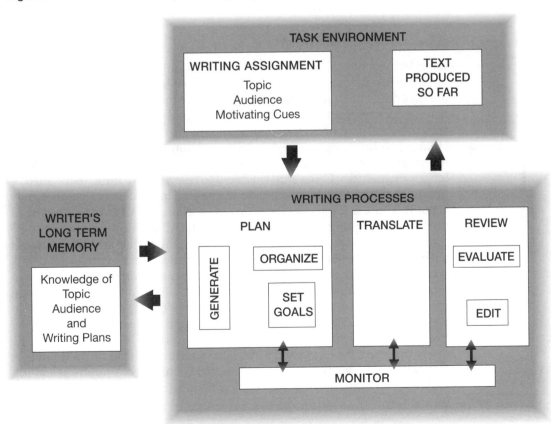

The task environment

Flower and Hayes use the term 'the rhetorical problem' in their model to refer to the challenge facing the writer, either in response to an assigned topic or one coming from his/her own interests, to write something which meets the aims of the assignment, satisfies the audience and accommodates the writer's own goals. Thus, an assignment on the rise of the Civil Rights movement in the USA should not stray too widely and contain too much information about American jazz of the 1960s which, however much it may be a particular passion of the writer, will not meet the goals of the assignment or its audience. Or a letter intended to console a friend about a failed examination should not include any reference to the writer's own successes. The rhetorical problem is a juggling act for the writer who has to keep an eye on a number of balls in the air simultaneously.

The text as it is being written acts as a guide to what needs to be done next. Each sentence is shaped by its predecessor and, in turn, shapes the following sentence. A particular anecdote or turn of phrase that appeals to the writer may turn the entire thrust of the writing in a totally different direction to that originally planned by the writer. Replanning may then be required.

 Long-term memory

Long-term memory contains not only relevant information which the writer has stored in the past about the topic, but also knowledge about where to obtain additional information that the writer may need. This information may be derived from books, magazines and newspapers, or may have been seen on television, or on video, or at the movies or have been gained from talking to other people. The difficulty with long-term memory is twofold. Information has to be accessed from the vast store of information held in long-term memory. Often students need to be primed to bring to the surface the information that is relevant to the task. They don't realise that they actually know a lot about dogs, or house plans, or air travel. They need time and prompting to remind them. Secondly, the information has to be transformed to meet the immediate needs of the writer and the reader. It will need to be reorganised, perhaps reworded and shorn of irrelevant detail. A common mistake many students make under examination pressure is to retrieve all the information they know about a topic and fail to transform the information to answer the specific needs of the question. Thus, an assignment about Captain Cook's first voyage to the South Pacific may trigger a flow of information about Cook's birth, his ship, his scientific discoveries and his death and yet fail to describe in detail his first voyage. Throughout the writing exercise, then, the writer is continually searching the contents of long-term memory, and making decisions about its relevance for the task.

The process at work

The most important component in the model focuses on the processes of planning, translating and rewriting. **Planning** is not just jotting down a few ideas, but has broader connotations for Flower and Hayes. They describe it as 'forming an internal representation of the knowledge that will be used in writing' (p. 372). It is more common in mature writers than in children. Planning can be undertaken in the form of words or sentences but it can also take the form of pictures or sounds in the mind of the writer which must later be transformed into words. Indeed, planning is broken into three subsections – 'generating ideas', which includes searching one's memory banks for relevant ideas, 'organising' which fits the ideas generated into a coherent structure, and 'goal setting'. The latter is seen as an on-going process whereby particular goals generate new ideas which in turn lead to new goals being set. Flower and Hayes (1981, p. 373) consider that

> 'the act of developing and refining one's own goals is not limited to a "pre-writing stage" in the composing process, but is intimately bound up with the on-going, moment-to-moment process of composing.'

So the goals of the mature writer are tentative, rather than fixed. But planning is an important stage, which is neglected by young writers and too often means disorganised or unbalanced products.

Translating involves putting one's ideas down on paper. It involves the conscious putting of one's thoughts into suitable words and structures, using the conventions of print that are appropriate to the message, and at the same time making sure that the content of the message has not been sacrificed to the demands of these surface dimensions of print. If students are too worried about the consequences of spelling errors or inadequate handwriting, the flow of ideas and the quality of the content does suffer.

Reviewing consists of two sub-processes – evaluating and revising. Writers need to look critically at their efforts, and once they have evaluated the product, they need to have strategies for revision. Both of these sub-processes can occur at any time in the writing and are not necessarily confined to a separate action when the translating has finished.

Overseeing all of these processes is a function Flower and Hayes have called the *Monitor*. This is the mechanism whereby the writer switches from planning to translating, perhaps back to planning or on to revising. It's the controller (Flower and Hayes use the term 'executive routine') of all the processes and determines which process will be used at a particular time.

The cognitive process model is not a tidy sequence of steps to be followed in a pre-determined order. It is a dynamic model where writers switch between steps at any stage in response to the demands made upon them by the particular piece of writing, by their perception of audience, and by the cues which occur to them as they write.

It is a model which grew out of the researchers' comparisons of expert and novice writers, retold to them in interviews with the students during or immediately after the writing process. However, it has little to say about how the students move from novice to expert status. Furthermore, they appear to ignore the fact that the writing processes do vary according to context – to the task set, the goals of the writers and their culture (see Applebee et al., 1986).

 ## Summary

In an elaboration of their model, Flower and Hayes (1984) suggest that their model of writing as a cognitive process buries two popular myths about writing. The first is that setting words down on paper is a process akin to a tropical storm, where, after a humid period of brooding weather, the writer suddenly pours down the words onto the page without thought or preparation in a deluge of writing. Flower and Hayes explain that in a case such as this, there has been a considerable period of conscious thinking about the writing but much of this thinking may not be recognised by the writer as thinking about writing. Unlike tropical storms, writing does not suddenly spring out of an empty sky.

The second myth is to see putting words on paper as a relentless, step-by-step march from ideas to words to prose during which authors first get ideas straight in their mind, then translate the ideas into words and finally record the words on paper. Writers can begin anywhere – with an idea, a turn of phrase, an emotion, an image and shuttle back and forth between ideas, images, emotions and words.

 ## The switch from conversation to composition: insights from the experimental research of Bereiter and Scardamalia

Our understanding of the problems children face in learning to write like experts was given a major boost in the 1980s with the experimental research programme of Carl Bereiter and Marlene Scardamalia (1982; 1983) in Toronto, Canada.

These researchers argued that novice pupils learning to write face a series of challenges that they must cope with before they can become the fluent, expert writers that are assumed in the model of Flower and Hayes.

The first of these is the problem of switching from oral to graphic expression. Children learn to talk naturally, and by school age most are competent speakers. Learning to write, however, requires them to learn a whole new set of conventions and skills, how to hold a pen, to write words, to spell them correctly, to mark pauses with commas and full stops, to group sentences into paragraphs, and so on. This transition from the oral to the graphic is an obvious one, which dominates many classroom programmes. However, it is not the only one.

The second challenge, according to Bereiter and Scardamalia, is that of moving from face-to-face communication to communication with a remote audience, an audience which requires the writer to exercise new levels of abstract thought. At the point of writing, the young writer must try to put himself/herself in the potential readers' shoes, anticipate their needs and write in such a way that they can comprehend without the benefit of the writer's gestures, of facial expression or physical pointing. The message has to be self-contained.

Thirdly, there is the challenge of writing without the stimulus of feedback from a conversational partner. The writer must learn to generate text without regular comments or questions from a listener. In this sense, the text has to be autonomous. It is this third transition that prompted much of the research programme of Bereiter and Scardamalia.

What does it mean to write autonomous text, without the assistance of a conversational partner? Bereiter and Scardamalia (1982) have identified four kinds of problems that young writers face when they set out on the lonely road to composition, without the usual friendly feedback.

1   Learning to produce continuous text without a turn-taking partner

Too often the young writer stops after one point has been made. They need someone to prompt them to continue with nods, questions and comments – like 'Really?' and 'Yes, of course,' and 'How did you feel?'.

2   Learning to search one's memory to generate more suitable content

Young children appear to have no system to help them think of something relevant, even though they may have much passive information waiting to be retrieved. They need memory aids and prompts.

3   Learning to think ahead, to plan beyond the present sentence

It is natural to focus on the problems of expressing this sentence, here and now, without worrying about the next paragraph or the overall plan. Young writers can't see the wood for the trees.

4   Learning to revise one's own writing

During the redrafting process, children seem to be dominated by the actual words they have written, and are unable to visualise other, better ways of expressing their thoughts. They cannot readily shift from writing to evaluating. There is too much requiring their attention.

It is easy for adult, experienced writers to overlook these challenges which the beginner has to overcome. But perhaps there are new ways of helping them do so.

Mini-experiments designed to overcome children's problems

In a series of ingenious, small-scale interventions, Bereiter and Scardamalia and their colleagues in the Toronto Writing School set out to help the young writer confront these problems, and evaluated each of their interventions with simple writing exercises. Not all of them were successful, but the neat simplicity of their studies and the potential insights they offer teachers of writing will amply repay a study of them.

1 Learning to generate continuous text without a respondent

Experienced writers generate more text than beginners, not necessarily because the latter have less to say, but because the multiple challenges of handwriting, spelling and punctuation are all-absorbing and tiring. Beginners seem to need the regular prompting of a conversational partner to keep them focused. Not surprisingly, they often 'dry up' quickly after one or two sentences especially when writing on non-narrative topics. In one study, quoted by Bereiter and Scardamalia (1982), Hidi and Hildyard compared the oral and written expression of primary school children on narrative topics and opinion topics. On average, the pupils generated much longer products in the oral mode than the written one, (90 words versus 60 words), and more in the narrative mode than when expressing their opinion (110 words versus 43 words).

For instance, when writing on the question 'Should boys and girls play in the same sports teams?', nine- and ten-year-olds typically wrote one sentence and then stopped. Older children usually managed two points. The pattern was that of a conversational turn, awaiting a reaction. They were stuck in conversational mode.

First of all Bereiter and Scardamalia (1982) tested the hypothesis that the clumsiness of the physical act of writing slowed the children down, and that they would write more continuous text if someone else did the writing for them. The researchers compared three modes – **speaking**, **dictating to a scribe** and **writing** – all on the same opinion topic. As predicted, children produced most when speaking (average = 45 words); next when dictating (35 words) and least when writing under usual conditions (20 words). Having someone else take over the psycho-motor burden of transferring their words on to paper did help the production process.

A second hypothesis was that the lack of prompting from a conversational partner could be overcome by having the teacher/supervisor regularly prompting the writer with 'contentless prompts' – general statements to keep going, such as 'Go on', 'I'd like to know more about that', 'Tell us more'.

The researchers established three conditions:

1 Normal instructions to write an essay.

2 Instructions to write 'as much as possible'.

3 Instructions to write 'as much as possible' followed up with contentless prompts.

The researchers found that the second group produced three times as much material as the control group, while the third group produced almost twice as much again.

Apparently, beginning writers can produce more, given these aids to prompt them. The benefit of extra prompting, however, was much stronger than that of having a scribe to take over the physical act of writing. In fact, in a later article, Scardamalia and Bereiter (1986) reduced their emphasis on problems associated with the physical act. The small advantage obtained in quality of dictated essays was reversed when children were merely urged to carry on writing. A slower rate of production seemed to produce better quality than the quick burst typical of speaking and dictating. With experience, the physical actions do become automatic, but with very young children it is surely an inhibiting force.

Thus, the problem of generating extended text is a real one for younger writers. However, a system of contentless prompts, plus general encouragement to continue, and a sympathetic understanding of the reasons for a slow rate of production seem to be called for by the research. As pupils gain in experience, the physical production processes become automatic, allowing more time for thinking to become more focused.

2 Learning to search one's memory for more content

One reason why children 'dry up' when writing is their inability to recall what they already know for an essay. How can they retrieve relevant information when their limited attention span is so fully occupied with the other levels and tasks of writing? In conversation, children rarely need to do a memory search to think of something to say. One elephant joke reminds them of another; one embarrassing moment activates memories of a similar one; one sports achievement jogs their memory for another. They rarely need to switch and take up another topic cold. That is not how conversations proceed. Moreover, the actual process of speaking rarely requires conscious attention in the way that writing does.

Many teachers do assist pupils with this transition by conducting pre-writing sessions. If the essay topic is about the merits of wearing school uniforms, they may set up a class discussion, list arguments for and against, encourage children to tell a few anecdotes, write a blackboard summary, quote from a book, or record some helpful enriching vocabulary. All such activities are calculated to facilitate memory search and bring relevant ideas to the surface.

In their research, Bereiter and Scardamalia predicted that a pre-writing 'brainstorming' session would help pupils retrieve more relevant ideas to write about. Children aged 9–13 years were given a topic and asked to think about it, and then write down whatever thoughts occurred to them, whether they seemed helpful or not – a kind of green light period where anything goes. They could then review what they had written, and decide what to use. Under these circumstances, the brainstorming strategy was not very successful. In the event, the pupils tended to write whole sentences and found it a clumsy procedure. Perhaps an oral brainstorming session would have served them better.

The second strategy produced more benefits. Rather than write out complete sentences, the children worked as a group to **produce lists of words** that were relevant to the topic. On the subject of school uniforms they might produce words like *expensive, loyalty, tradition, pride, competition* – just enough to remind pupils of a point to make or an argument to develop.

A trip-to-the-moon topic could be enriched by listing such words as *astronaut, count-down, spaceship, blast-off, weightlessness, eerie, wonder*. After 12 training sessions, Toronto Grade 6 pupils who used this word-listing approach generated twice as much writing as control groups writing on the same topic; they also used three times as many unusual words, included 50% more arguments for their viewpoint, and elaborated their arguments better. In terms of the aim of the project, the pupils were able to develop an efficient memory search routine which helped them bring relevant ideas to the surface. There is no guarantee that the writing will be of better quality, as the results of the researchers' evaluations did not find significant improvement in quality. However, with more content to work on, and the confidence that comes with a successful memory search, the long-term prospects for improvement would surely be enhanced.

In another experiment, pupils were asked to describe the rules of a new game they had watched on video. Most high school students were able to write a full and adequate description (mean = 20 out of 23 ideas). By contrast, younger pupils (Grade 4) were unable to organise their memory search at all well, finishing with only eight of the relevant points to make – insufficient for an audience of learners to understand. So the researchers set up a classroom experiment with another group of Grade 4 children. The rationale was that pupils needed help to organise their memory search from the point of view of the learner of the game. The experimental group saw the same video of the game once, then watched a second video in which the instructions for the game were totally inadequate, leading only to confusion for the learner. Then, they wrote their own description. Meanwhile, a control group saw the original video of the game twice. As predicted, the inadequate video served the purpose of prompting the pupils to recall many more of the rules needed to understand the game. It seems that they actually knew the information, but needed help to retrieve it and to see where and why it was relevant.

This series of experiments appears to confirm the importance of helping young children to find ways of searching their memory files as an aid to generation of content for a writing exercise, when a conversational partner is not around to prompt them, and to keep them on track.

Many of the suggestions listed above should be helpful – providing word lists, discussing pros and cons, encouraging anecdotes, conferencing and generally sharing ideas, before and during writing, are all potential aids to memory search.

3 Learning to think ahead, to plan beyond the present sentence

From their observations and interviews with children in the act of writing, Bereiter and Scardamalia noted that many of them were unable to think in terms of an overall plan or goal for their writing. They moved from one example to the next, in rambling fashion, without visualising where they wanted to get to. They indulged in what Bereiter and Scardamalia referred to as 'knowledge telling'. 'What I know about horses is this...' without structure or plan. This problem of shifting from 'local' to 'whole-text' planning is another part of the overall challenge of writing autonomous text without a conversational partner. It probably reflects a natural limitation of young children's working memory. They cannot think about several things at once. They cannot generate an idea, transform it into words, and test it for appropriateness as adults can.

To help pupils overcome this problem, Bereiter and Scardamalia experimented with strategies in which they provided pupils with lists of possible sentence openers that would help them through the complete story or argument that they were developing. For example:

The first reason why…
Secondly…
A third factor…
On the other hand, some people…
To sum up…

Another strategy was to provide pupils with a topic to write about, and possible endings to their composition, endings which required them to plan. For instance, when the topic was 'The Duke and the Vampire', the suggested ending was 'And so, after considering the reasons for it, and the reasons against it, the duke decided to rent his castle to the vampire after all, in spite of the rumour he had heard'.

To write an essay that led to such a conclusion, pupils had to consider many elements before they started to write. Some children did benefit from such a procedure, but many still resorted to 'local' writing, with no coherent overall plan. The researchers concluded that interventions that have a significant effect on main ideas and goal formation 'remain to be demonstrated' (Scardamalia and Bereiter, 1986, p. 790). They did see some hope in the conferencing techniques advocated by Graves. However, they doubted whether many teachers had developed enough insight into the processes of good writing to help their pupils in this way (Bereiter and Scardamalia, 1983).

4   Learning to revise one's own writing

Many researchers have studied students' attempts to revise their own writing, and the results have not been spectacular. Most students do little more than proofread at a superficial level (Bereiter and Scardamalia, 1983), and increased amounts of revision rarely improve quality. Most revisions are limited to the addition of commas, correcting spelling, and word choice and not to restructuring or adding sections to help the reader. Redrafting is not a process used in speaking, and when children attempt it in writing they seem unable to go beyond the words they have already written.

The Toronto researchers hypothesised that children were constrained by Piaget's concept of an inability to 'decentre', to put themselves in others' shoes. 'If I can understand it, surely you can!' This theory was tested by asking children to revise other pupils' essays, or to wait a week and try to revise their own. Even then, when the readers had to surmise what the writer had intended, their revisions were superficial.

Bereiter's interpretation was that the children's problems were again due to the lack of feedback from a partner. They had no built-in feedback system that allowed them to switch roles to that of the partner evaluating what was being written. Would an artificial feedback system work?

The researchers devised a new intervention in the shape of revision cards, designed to provide feedback (see Table 4). Each card contained a single statement that a teacher or a conversational partner might make, either to evaluate the sentence or to direct them to a better way of stating the sentence. In one study, pupils wrote their story, then re-read it, stopping after each sentence to select an appropriate evaluative card with a statement which fitted the sentence. In a second study, the pupils used the cards while they were in the act of composing their first drafts.

Both studies showed promise. Pupils agreed that the cue cards helped them improve their writing, and independent judges agreed with their revisions most of the time. However, the researchers concluded that pupils needed more practice with such a strategy if their essays were to show overall improvement. In large classes, where teacher conferencing is irregular for many pupils, a revision card system could well find a useful role.

Conclusion

Bereiter and Scardamalia have followed up this line of research with further attempts to overcome the child's difficulties in coping with several tasks simultaneously – before they become automatic. These small-scale classroom experiments have clarified the kinds of problems children have, and helped teachers to see possible ways of improving their interactions with their students before, during and after they write. If teachers recognise the particular limitations children have, and can work out which can be overcome with natural or artificial aids and which are inherent in their pupils' immature working memories, they can save much frustration both for themselves and their children.

Table 4 – Sample statements on revision cards (Bereiter and Scardamalia, 1982)

1   Evaluative cards
People won't see why this is significant.
People may not understand this.
This doesn't sound quite right.
This is good.

2   Directing Cards
I'd better give an example.
I'd better say more.
I'd better change the wording.

An applied behavioural approach to writing instruction

'Without doubt, the teacher's enthusiastic response to a student's writing is the most powerful stimulus to motivate students and encourage further quality work.'
D. Bates, (1994) Revise, Edit and Rewrite

Writing is a form of behaviour. For some children it becomes a regular habit; for others it is something to be avoided. Most teachers and parents would like to push children gently towards seeing writing as a desirable form of behaviour. How is this best done? One group of educational psychologists who focus on the way our behavioural patterns develop and change have conducted a number of useful studies which can help us to understand how to arrange conditions so that pupils will indeed write more willingly and more often. They study the particular circumstances which surround children's writing, change them systematically and observe carefully how they affect children's writing behaviour.

This chapter outlines the rationale for a behavioural approach to writing instruction, and some of the research studies which have investigated ways in which adults can change children's writing behaviour. We draw heavily on the work of Professor Ted Glynn and his students and colleagues in Auckland and Dunedin, New Zealand.

What is the applied behavioural rationale?

Behaviourists emphasise the role of the environment in 'shaping' our behaviour. Children's habits are strongly influenced – some would say determined – by what happens to them when they behave in particular ways. If they are praised, or 'reinforced' for an activity, in a particular way, they will repeat this action. When baby Beth first says 'Mama', Mother laughs, repeats 'Mama', cuddles Beth and makes her feel she has done something great. So Beth will probably say it again. When Harry calls out in class with a clever comment that makes everybody laugh, he soon repeats his behaviour, even if it earns him a reprimand from his teacher. These actions are 'reinforced' by the feedback they receive from their social environment. The behaviour of Beth and Harry is affected by how people respond to what they do. It seems that people's behaviour is very sensitive to the immediate social environment.

Behaviourists have studied the way in which different kinds of social responding affect the behaviour of children and animals, and shown how student writing is also subject to particular environmental influences. The way in which parents respond to their preschoolers' first efforts, and the way in which teachers evaluate their students' drafts have a great deal to do with their willingness to put further effort into their writing sessions and with their propensity to take charge of their own writing in the future. It is important, then, that we adults try to understand the complex links between children's writing behaviour and how we respond to it. In this school of thought, the type of feedback we give to children is crucial.

Responding to young children's writing at home

Chapter 3 described the development of writing in the early childhood years. Most young children appear to have a strong motivation to communicate in writing. In a New Zealand survey of 79 children who were experiencing difficulty in learning to read, Glynn et al. (1989) found that as many as 60 of them were regular writers at home, and the parents of 19 of the children reported that their children tried to write something every day. Typically, they liked to write their names (80%), to write stories (55%), letters (50%), greeting cards (55%), and to copy specific letters and words (72%). Most parents reported that these were child-initiated activities, which they enjoyed performing. Yet many were not enthusiastic about writing at school, and reported very little directed homework writing.

In an effort to explore the differences between home and school environments for fostering the writing habit, Arndt (1980) made an extended study of a seven-year-old Auckland child (who will be called Margaret). Margaret's teacher found her unwilling to write at school. She would write only 3–5 words in ten minutes, yet her other language skills were well advanced.

Arndt observed Margaret's writing eight times for ten-minute periods, both at home and at school during a *baseline* period (i.e., a period which showed what she would typically do without any intervention). This phase of the study showed that Margaret wrote nearly three times as much at home, under her mother's supervision, as she did at school (24.0 words compared to 8.9 words per ten minutes). Yet the accuracy of her letter formation was very similar in both locations. Arndt assumed that something in the social environment must have been responsible for the large difference in the amount she wrote.

Next, Arndt decided to change the context of the home sessions, in an effort to improve even further the amount of writing that Margaret did. Before she wrote anything, Margaret's mother discussed with her what she might write, and after she had finished her writing, her mother commented positively on what she had written – both the amount and the content. In addition, she read the story aloud to another adult, and typed out her stories to keep in a special folder. With this kind of positive feedback (or reinforcement) for her efforts, Margaret's writing rate almost doubled for every ten minute period, and the accuracy of her writing improved dramatically, from 37.5% to 67.9%. This was despite that fact that her mother gave her no help with letter formation.

However, and this was surprising, there was virtually no change in Margaret's writing at school. While her rate at home improved from 24.0

words to 40.8 words per ten-minute period, her rate at school improved by only 2.1 words. While her accuracy at home changed by 30.3%, her accuracy at school improved by only 7.5%.

Why was there so little change at school? Observation showed that Margaret received little positive feedback for her writing at school, and that she was easily distracted by others, in a situation where the teacher's attention had to be divided among 30 restless children. Such an unproductive environment could be changed by using parents or teacher aides who are able to provide a more systematic regime of feedback and positive attention to a child's individual efforts at communicating in writing. Arndt's study showed that a parent can have a marked impact on a child's writing behaviour at home by modifying the key factors that affect the child's behaviour. It also underlines the point that children's skills will vary according to the context (home or school), and that homes are potentially more productive than schools for teaching some writing skills (see Chapter 4).

Can everyone be taught to write?

In another experiment conducted in Auckland, Glynn et al. (1975) showed how a group of nine intellectually challenged children aged between seven and nine, from a special class, could learn to write under a behaviourally managed system of incentives. At the outset, these nine pupils, with IQs in the 60–75 range, were unable to write independently.

The researchers observed the classroom and noted that the teacher rarely provided helpful feedback in the children's writing sessions, largely due to the excessive amount of disruptive behaviour. And, while the children were able to copy words and letters, they did not write any words or sentences of their own.

During a baseline period of 40 days, the researchers closely studied the typical circumstances of their writing behaviour. They classified the children's behaviour as 'on task' (doing what was expected) or 'off task' (doing something else). The researchers also coded the children's writing efforts into four categories: copying (on the same page); transcribing to another page; producing own words; producing own sentences.

The average amount of on-task writing behaviour for these children in the baseline period was only 65% and 64.4% respectively for two 40-day periods. At this point, the researchers introduced two changes using an incentive system. Points were awarded by the teacher for two kinds of behaviour. All nine pupils received a common number of points for the average rate of on-task behaviour of the whole class in their writing lessons. In addition, each pupil received extra points for individual work. These points earned the children extra time to play with a wide array of games, toys and puzzles.

The check for 'on-task' behaviour was managed by means of a tape-recorder, which emitted 12 beeps per writing lesson (two to five minutes apart). When the beep was heard, the teacher scanned the class. If all were engaged in the appropriate behaviour (writing) she would record a group tick on the blackboard. If some were off-task, she said nothing and recorded no tick. At the end of the lesson, pupils recorded the number of ticks (points) earned in a small notebook. To earn credit for individual writing achievement, the pupils received one point for each word copied or transcribed, two points for each self-produced word, and three points for a sentence. Correct spelling and letter formation were not necessary to earn points. The teacher gave credit for approximations to the desired behaviour, which is a key feature of behavioural systems.

After 16 weeks of this scheme, on-task behaviour rose from 65% to 77% then to 85%. It remained steady throughout the following year, above 80% (see Table 5). This context produced a much better learning environment for both teacher and pupils. It was noted that the teacher's comments on behaviour changed from an even balance of positive and negative at the outset, to a strong predominance of positive comments at the end of the study.

Meanwhile, the pupils' production of self-generated words and sentences improved from zero, during the two 40-day baseline periods, to an average of 31.9 words and 2.4 sentences per child at the end of the third 40-day period. At that stage it was agreed that no points would be awarded for merely copying or transcribing, (except for two pupils), and the number of words and sentences increased again. The pupils no longer needed the playroom incentives to keep them on task. During the following year, follow-up studies showed even further gains, as Table 5 shows.

Table 5 – Gains shown by nine pupils during behavioural incentive system (adapted from Glynn et al., 1975)

	Baseline		Follow-up				
Number of days	0–40	41–80	81–120	121–160	200	240	280
% on-task	65.0	64.4	77.4	84.5	81.3	80.8	88.0
Number of words	0.0	0.0	31.9	58.1	40.7	61.1	90.5
Number of sentences	0.0	0.0	2.4	8.0	6.9	9.1	12.5

By the end of the study, all nine pupils were able to generate sentences on their own, yet none could produce single words at the beginning. During the early stages of the intervention the children's sentences were very simple, e.g. 'I am a boy. My name is Terry'.

However, towards the end, the researchers noted a number of complex sentences appearing amongst the simpler ones, e.g. 'If a bee comes along and there was a boy standing there, the boy would run away'.

Furthermore, the pupils' attitude towards writing changed from negative to positive. They looked forward to writing times and enjoyed sharing their efforts with others.

Four conclusions seem warranted from this study.

1   Intellectually challenged pupils can learn to write if the teachers respond appropriately to their efforts.

2   A system of positive feedback produces greater improvements than a system which emphasises negative comments.

3   If children are given credit for approximations to the correct forms, they will gradually improve. Fluency is more important than accuracy in the early stages.

4   As children progress they seem to depend less on an external feedback system.

Increasing the writing rate of low-achieving secondary school students

As we saw in Chapter 4, many secondary students write very little original prose at school, and too many are reluctant to write at all. A behavioural analysis suggests that they receive too little feedback for their efforts, and what they do receive is often delayed and frequently unhelpful, with a heavy emphasis placed on fault-finding (Scriven and Glynn, 1983). Accuracy often takes precedence over fluency. Some studies have shown that such an emphasis has a negative impact. Students write less than before, if the feedback they get is inappropriate (Ferritor et al., 1972; Marholin and Steinman, 1977).

In a study of 27 students in a multi-ethnic low-achieving fourth form class (Year 10) of an urban secondary school, Scriven and Glynn (1983) set out to investigate the impact of increased feedback on the students' writing rate, accuracy and task completion. The study focused on **prose writing**, **skills** (summaries, graphs, maps) and short **structured items** (matching, sentence completion tasks) in the students' English and Social Studies classes. During the baseline period, the researchers observed the classes and recorded the teachers' positive and negative comments in class. They also coded the students' on-task behaviour, writing rate and task completion. During the intervention phase, these figures were displayed prominently on a large chart. The teacher regularly drew attention to them with positive remarks about students' improvements. After the baseline period, the feedback system was introduced (phase 2) for **prose writing** only. The effects on students' prose writing during this phase were observed to change markedly, from about three words written per minute to more than nine words. Accuracy, too, improved, from 84% to 92%, while the percentage of prose tasks completed changed from 77% to 88%. Little or no change occurred in the corresponding figures for skills and structured items, which had received no special feedback.

After another three-and-a-half weeks, the teacher introduced the feedback system for **skills** as well as **prose writing**, (phase 3) and a parallel jump occurred in the average student's speed, accuracy and task completion rates for skills. Finally, in phase 4, the intervention was applied to **structured items**, with corresponding gains in those activities. Meanwhile, students' on-task behaviour rose steadily from 67% in the baseline period to 85% in phase 4, and teacher comments on behaviour became proportionally more positive.

The researchers concluded that the positive feedback improved the students' rate of performance dramatically, and that their accuracy and task completion improved at the same time. There was no loss of quality as the quantity of their writing increased. While the feedback system used may be too time-consuming for many teachers to implement, its effects were so strong that the researchers recommended that teacher aides or a school's clerical staff could be well used in a classroom that was using this system. Once sufficient gains had been registered, most students should soon be able to manage their own feedback systems without further help.

How should teachers respond to children's writing?

Parents of young effective writers are very responsive to their children's efforts. They sit with them, try to understand what they are trying to express and respond personally to the message.

In a study of 24 nine- to ten-year-olds in an Auckland school, Jerram et al. (1988) investigated the effects of providing written feedback to each child. The teacher used a modified process writing approach, (see Chapter 6), in which pupils wrote for 15 minutes on self-selected topics, and did not stop to ask for difficult spellings. They 'had a go'. The teacher adopted a positive, interested approach during the writing sessions, but avoided specific oral comments on pupil writing.

After a three-week baseline period, the teacher introduced a written feedback system for two weeks. She wrote specific positive comments on each child's writing, similar to those suggested by Graves (1983) in teacher-pupil conferences – e.g., personal feelings about characters, themes, anticipation of things to come, conversing with the writer, addressing the writer by name. No faults were identified, or corrective suggestions made at all.

As predicted, the feedback system had a clear-cut impact on the quantity and quality of the children's writing. The rate of writing improved from 72 to 91 words per session; the spelling (of the poor spellers) rose from 96.4% correct to 99.8%, and ratings of quality made by parents and educators showed marked improvement. Moreover, the pupils were writing on more imaginative themes and using a wider range of vocabulary.

To see whether the effects were stable, the teacher stopped the feedback system for three days. Immediately, the children returned to typical baseline behaviour – or even lower. So the teacher reintroduced the system for another two weeks, and the children's behaviour improved again, both in quantity and quality. Their stories became longer and more continuous from day to day. Clearly, the personal written comments on the children's writing had a quick and beneficial impact.

A similar study of 31 secondary school students (11–13 years) was conducted by Logan and Glynn (1989). This time, there was a positive but less consistent impact on the actual number of words that the students wrote in class sessions. However, there was a substantial impact on quality. Six professional educators selected and rated samples of the students' writing for their general interest and reader impact. For the two baseline phases the average ratings totalled 19 and 15 points; for the two feedback phases they improved to 23 and 23. Once again, the focus on content rather than form resulted in quality gains.

The pattern of results for the number of words written was complicated by the fact that these students gained alternative sources of feedback from their peers, whose influence is stronger for older children than for younger ones. Furthermore, the writing of the secondary school students covered a wide range of genres, from poems, to diaries, checklists, plays and extended prose – so that again the number of words written was an unreliable index of progress. Some pupils actually spent their time writing personal comments on the teacher's feedback rather than producing a conventional prose piece.

Nevertheless, the impact of written personal feedback on pupil writing behaviour was confirmed by this study. For the teacher, the most impressive outcome was the greatly increased enthusiasm for writing in her class. Non-judgemental feedback apparently produced an environment which was less arduous and more fun. Moreover, she did not find the written comment system any more time-consuming than traditional marking.

Helping reluctant writers towards independence

Some classrooms are unsuitable environments for developing independent writing behaviour because of the high level of disruptive behaviour. It is difficult for teachers to be supportive and positive in their comments when they are preoccupied with restricting and punishing. Studies of pupils in such classrooms, however, show that an applied behavioural approach can bring about positive changes.

For instance, Rumsey and Ballard (1985) studied seven disruptive pupils in a primary school class of 34 children. The researchers used two different behavioural systems to bring these seven pupils towards more productive classroom behaviour and independent writing. First, they developed a self-recording scheme. The teacher played an audio-tape during writing sessions. The tape produced audible tones, between one and five minutes apart. Whenever a signal sounded, pupils recorded on a chart whether or not they were working. At the end of the session they also recorded how many words they had written.

The second strategy, called 'correspondence training,' involved personal interviews with each student. First, the teacher showed them a list of four target behaviours on a chart (e.g., 'I will try to write a really good story' 'I will not talk to others') which the pupils tried to memorise. After the lesson, the teacher discussed with each student the **extent** of **correspondence** between the target behaviours and the behaviours recorded during the session. If they achieved their targets they were warmly praised.

Both strategies proved effective. As a result of the self-recording strategy, on-task (working) behaviour increased from 38% to 66%, and quantity of writing increased from 48 to 140 words. After a return to baseline, and a second self-recording phase, the correspondence training was introduced. This, in turn, led to further gains of 18% in on-task behaviour and 45 words in writing.

In a similar study of correspondence training, with four low-achieving 14-year-old boys (Hopman and Glynn, 1989), the researchers had each boy nominate the number of words they could write in a lesson. Afterwards, they discussed the level of correspondence between the target number and the actual numbers completed, and reinforced them, where appropriate, with positive comments. Higher targets were then set. The focus was kept on targets and feedback for quantity, without regard for grammar or spelling, since earlier studies showed that quality improvements went hand-in-hand with increased volume of writing.

Once again, correspondence training proved very effective. Not only did the boys' writing improve in quantity (from a mean of 59 to 100 words written) as a result of correspondence training, but the writing also showed marked gains in quality. Vocabulary breadth improved by 66%; creativity ratings improved by 61%; sentence complexity improved by 59% and there was no increase in spelling or grammatical errors as a result of the students' more adventurous writing. Moreover, these gains proved stable when the classroom teacher took over from the researchers and during a maintenance period after the teacher stopped discussing the results with the pupils, and merely had them set targets for themselves. The boys were then well on the way to becoming competent independent writers.

Another study showed how students' independence in writing can be phased in, in such a way that teachers are not 'run off their feet' with too many demands for help with spelling. In the project with intellectually challenged primary school pupils discussed above, the improved writing shown by the children was found to be very demanding for the teacher who could not keep up with requests for spelling. To investigate alternatives, Wilson and Glynn (1983) worked with five pupils from this class who showed excessive levels of dependence on the teacher.

The researchers developed a list of 104 frequently requested words. They arranged the words alphabetically, by topic, and distributed one to each child. For four writing sessions pupils attempted to use the word lists. Then the researchers introduced a second phase – teacher praise for appropriate use of the lists. This went on for five sessions. Then they stepped up the reward systems by using cards to record the number of words that had to be supplied by the teacher. Sweets were given for uncrossed squares on the card. Too many requests for help (i.e. uncrossed squares) meant a penalty – no sweets.

Under this behavioural regime the pupils continued to write at the same levels of quantity and quality, but they became steadily less dependent. For the teacher, this was an important feature. Pupils now found 93% of their own words, compared with 77% during the baseline sessions. Each new strategy led to an improvement in independence. The teacher's effort was now transferred from telling children what to write, to independence training. Students were gradually becoming autonomous writers in charge of their own behaviour.

Cameron, Depree, Walker and Moore (1991) demonstrated that children tutoring each other was an effective way of improving the quality of children's writing. In this experiment, the writing progress of 16 pairs of children, one of whom was the tutor and the other the 'tutee' or person tutored, was compared with that of 20 children who were given additional opportunities to practise writing, but no tutoring. The experimental groups were chosen from two classes of six-year-old and eight- to nine-year-old children, all of whom were experiencing difficulties with writing. Older children acted as tutors and were paired up with younger children.

Tutors received two half-hour training sessions, during which they learned to make positive comments to their tutees about their writing and to encourage them to write more. The tutoring programme operated on four days a week for seven weeks. Tutorial sessions were of 30 minutes' duration. Assessment measures included collecting a ten-minute writing sample from all children on a selected topic. The sample was assessed by independent judges.

The results were unequivocal. Significant improvements in writing measures, as well as reading measures, were demonstrated by all children. Analysis of the unassisted writing samples showed improvement in both quality and accuracy, for both tutors and tutees. The only difficulties tutors had was in applying accurate feedback on spelling.

This study is important because it shows that giving more time to writing is not, in itself, a sufficient condition for improving the quality and the quantity of writing. However, when time is coupled with assistance and feedback from peers, both tutor and tutee were shown to have improved their writing skills. Furthermore, the study showed that it is possible to teach young children how to respond positively to their peers' writing and to suggest ways in which it could be improved.

Responding to students' writing faults

The studies reported above lend support to the view that children will gradually eliminate their errors if they are given encouragement to write often, in a climate that is tolerant of their errors. Just as young children gradually learn to improve their own speech with practice, so young students will improve in spelling, grammar and style if they regularly strive to get across their personal message in writing, in a social environment where they feel that there is genuine communication and where others are responsive to the content of their message. They seem to improve most where they have confidence in the kind of responsive environment they inhabit.

However, some errors do tend to be repeated, and it is still important to guide students towards faultless writing in due course. A behavioural viewpoint suggests that this is best done sparingly and selectively, one point at a time, once students are working with fluency and confidence.

As Wheldall & Glynn (1989) point out, frequent fault finding only reduces children's output and their opportunity to grow. They need a responsive feedback system to establish the habit of writing. A responsive regime means allowing them as much control as possible over the writing process – when they write, what they write, how much they write and whom they write to. Comments by teachers on what they write should do nothing to discourage this growth towards fluency. Yet, so often, such comments do just that. Teachers underline every spelling and grammatical mistake, and give the student the message that writing is more about getting it exactly right, than about expressing one's thoughts.

For instance, excessive marking of spelling errors is likely to reduce a child's adventurousness in trying out new words. Logan and Glynn (1989) cite the example of Timothy who typically wrote about 25 different words, and made about five spelling errors (80% correct). When his output increased, under a responsive feedback system, to 95 words, with 15 errors per story, there was an improvement in rate to 84% correct. But too often, the teacher could be tempted to note only the increase in the number of spelling errors, from 5 to 15. What Timothy needs is more credit for being venturesome.

A better approach to improving spelling is to use a graded word list such as Arvidson's (1977) and have children work on learning a particular set of needed words until they are mastered – in spelling lessons, not writing. A good practice is to have pupils prepare their own lists and work on them. This method means that pupils can see a finite task completed, relevant to their current needs and earn a reward for growth. Words misspelt which are beyond their level are ignored until later (see Chapter 12 for further details).

Grammatical, capitalisation and punctuation faults can also be handled one or two at a time, and tailor-made to fit the needs of each student. Some teachers write comments to the writer using the correct forms. Others tell students they have made faults in lines 3 and 7 and ask them to identify and correct them, giving them a measure of control over their learning. The point is that errors do matter, but they should be targeted selectively, and opportunity given for praise when they are corrected.

Summary

The behavioural approach to writing instruction emphasises the key role of responsive feedback to the child's efforts. If teachers and parents can respond positively to the writer's message, the content, feelings and ideas expressed, then improvements in quantity and subsequently in quality will follow. Sometimes this approach requires prior attention to minimising disruptions and distractions. But once the students have been induced to write, by carefully designed management systems, they gradually gain control, they experiment with new forms of expression and gradually improve the quality of their writing. Competently organised behavioural systems, such as those outlined in this chapter, have much to contribute to improving our students' writing.

Writing across the curriculum

'There is something in the actual act of composing on paper that oils the juices of your cognitive processes, so that as you write, ideas take on meaning and shape'
A. Curruthers et al., (1991) The Word Process

It is fashionable today to separate learning to write from writing to learn. The belief is that once a child has learned to write, then writing can be used as a tool for learning. We consider that this division is too simplistic. Learning to write, like learning to read, is an infinite process that has no end. Every time we write something novel we are learning something more about the process of writing. As adult writers we may have mastered some of the surface features, such as acceptable grammar and spelling, although many skilled adult writers still make errors in these areas. But we still have to struggle anew with the content and style of our writing. How can a financially embarrassed parent write a letter to his 20-year-old son refusing him a loan to buy a car; how can an anxious mother write to her 22-year-old daughter to persuade her that hitch-hiking alone through Africa is not a good idea; how can a young secretary best write a complaint of sexual harassment at work and still keep her job? These are but a few of the examples where adult writers are faced with the complex task of writing and have to struggle to express their meanings clearly and delicately. No matter how proficient or how learned the writer, there are times when, as adults faced with a challenging writing task, we are in a similar state of mind to that of the seven-year-old having to write a letter of thanks to Grandma for the birthday present of a book that has already been read and not particularly enjoyed.

As children grow older and pass through the grade levels at school, the task that the teacher faces is to make them aware that writing is a multi-faceted tool which has a range of purposes and can be used in a range of ways. The danger, at first and in the early years, is that writing is seen as narrative writing and nothing else. Hood (1994, p. 6) comments about eight-year-old New Zealand children that 'Many (teachers and children) did not consider writing in science, health and social studies as "writing"'. We need to repair this situation.

New Zealand is not unique in its lack of attention to writing in all curriculum areas. Applebee (1981) observed classroom writing in two mid-western high schools in the USA, and also conducted a nation-wide survey of teachers in six subject areas – English, foreign languages, mathematics, science, social science and business education. The results showed that little class time was devoted to writing when one disregards time spent on 'mechanical' writing (copying, completing assignments) and informational writing (note taking). Thirteen years later, Spiegal, Andrews and Hoover (1994) found from a survey of 200 teachers in rural mid-western high schools, that little had changed since Applebee's work was published. With the exception of those who taught English, teachers required little original writing from students. Spiegal et al. conclude 'writing across the curriculum is not yet a reality in rural schools' (p. 15).

When children write in a variety of curriculum areas, according to Walker (1988), three things happen:

1   The children have a means of better understanding the content as they struggle to make sense of it and to produce coherent sentences.

2   They practise a technique which aids retention. Once they have actively processed the material in the act of writing, it is more likely to become a stable part of long-term memory.

3   They improve their writing skills in the curriculum area.

Each subject has its own style and particular demands, and practice is necessary to make them familiar. These are important advantages, which should encourage more writing in all the curriculum areas. However, Walker's claims should be interpreted cautiously. Only with appropriate instruction and feedback will these claims be justified. Sometimes children will practise the wrong thing or stress points of minor significance.

The role of genre

Genre refers to the organisation of writing at a level above sentences. Writing for particular purposes follows organisational patterns unique to that purpose. Letters to Grandmother and geography field-notes are organised differently. A letter of complaint, for example, should be factual, precise and avoid abuse. Science writing should be impersonal and objective. Directions on assembling kit-set furniture should be logically sequenced with numbered steps that proceed from the first step and culminate with the successfully assembled product. Not only the vocabulary, but also the syntax and the sentences themselves have to be organised in a way which people versed in the discipline will respond to in an appropriate way.

A complaints officer in Telecom, for instance, expects that letters of complaint will describe what happened, when and where. They will not respond to a diatribe about the costs of the service or the writer's financial position. Similarly, when reading a scientific report, readers will expect to read an objective description of the experiment or phenomena. They will be surprised if a report on the effects of continuous light on growing plants from a 16-year-old studying botany suddenly contains a poem of praise to the sun. We need, then, to ask how we can move children from writing only narrative – a common situation – to writing in a variety of genres. How can they make the transition from 'Goldilocks' to 'Caring for animals'? From 'Our boating holiday' to 'Safety at sea'?

Kress (1994) argues that learning genre is a way of socialising a child into appropriate and accepted ways of organising knowledge. To become an accepted member of the scientific community, one must write objectively, like a scientist. To write travel brochures, one must use quite a different style and vocabulary. Understanding genre is an integral part of learning mathematics or biology or science or English. Genres play an interesting role in our ability to write about what we have learned. In some instances, they form an important integrating structure which allows us to communicate easily with others who have similar interests. In other cases, they can blind us to new ways of seeing and responding and act as a conservative force. For example, scientific report writing has suppressed any mention of the personality of the writer and of his/her background. Yet, now some scientific thinkers are recognising that the background of the observer may dictate what the scientist observes and therefore how it is perceived.

Kress (1994) sees a conflict in education between creativity in language use and being a skilled writer in a particular genre. He writes 'the genre will construct the world for its proficient user. Is this what we want?' (p. 126). The genres most valued in school, Kress considers, are poetic and literary. He rightly asks whether these are the most important genres in the adult world. There is an obligation on teachers to expose children to the whole range of writing genres and to ease them gently and constructively into each one.

 ## Teaching genre

Is it possible to use direct teaching to enable children to write using a range of genres? The theme of Chapter 5 and the comments about the acquisition of oral language in Chapter 2 suggest that direct instruction is of little benefit in learning to write. Some researchers disagree. In Australia,

> *'a group of language educators who consider themselves Hallidayans have begun a concerted campaign to teach genres to children through explicit descriptions of a genre's rules and formal features beginning as early as the first years of elementary school.'*
> *(Freedman, 1993, p 223)*

Freedman (1993) questions whether such explicit teaching of genre is either useful or necessary. Indeed, she suggests that direct teaching of genre is impossible because we cannot specify all the rules by which writing in a particular genre is generated. Those features which can be stated explicitly are often very obvious and trivial. However, she suggests that under some conditions, some form of teacher guidance may be helpful. In support of the first part of her argument she quotes the prominent American linguist Krashen:

> *'The rules that describe written language… are simply too complex and too numerous to be explicitly taught and consciously learned.' (p. 232)*

Freedman describes two research studies she conducted to show that explicit teaching of genre structures is unnecessary. The first was an examination of the scripts of 7500 children in Grades 5, 8 and 12, which showed that the children had mastered an appropriate (and elaborate) story structure without formal instruction (Freedman, 1993). The second study was an examination of the writing of, and interviews with, six law students during the course of an introductory undergraduate course in law. She found that all the students mastered the complexities of writing legal essays for their course without the benefit of formal instruction in doing so. In fact, Freedman noted that the course instructors themselves were unable to specify in any detail what they were looking for when they graded the work.

Freedman's interpretation of the findings of both studies is that the context of the classes enabled the students to cope with the specialised writing. The discussions the students had with one another and with their instructors/teachers, together with the content offered during the classes and the reading that was required of them, combined to make formal instruction in writing in the appropriate genre unnecessary. Perhaps Freedman's findings are applicable only to successful students who go on to tertiary study.

The conclusion Freedman reaches from her work is that explicit teaching may be of some value when the students are involved in authentic tasks and authentic contexts. She describes these conditions thus (p. 244):

> 'Explicit discussions of the formal features of genre (always assuming the instructor's description is accurate) may prove useful for those students whose learning styles are appropriate, but only when such discussions are presented while students are engaged in authentic reading and writing tasks involving the targeted genre.'

We suggest that while explicit instruction in genre may be of little value, as Freedman so persuasively argues in her paper, children should still be encouraged to write in a range of subjects and in a range of styles. Regular classroom discussion of children's writing offers the opportunity to draw attention to some of the features of different genres. Hood (1995, p. 27) argues that they should be allowed 'to make independent discovery of the different genres and then be assisted to internalise the features through shared and guided writing'.

Anecdotal reports from teachers leave no doubt that children can be made aware of the difference between fiction and non-fiction as early as their first year at school. Perhaps this distinction is too elementary for researchers like Freedman to dignify with the label 'genre,' but we feel it is a significant step towards making children aware of differing prose styles. In Chapter 1, we saw how Katie was writing fluently in different genre by age ten. In fact, preschoolers use a range of genres in their oral language when they tell jokes, ask riddles and compile birthday guest-lists.

Duthie (1994), using Graves' process approach as a model, successfully taught her Grade 1 children to write non-fiction by reading non-fiction books, building up class lists of the characteristics of non-fiction writing in a series of mini-lessons, and by allowing the children to write about topics that were meaningful to them. One child, for instance, wrote an expository piece about teeth because 'I lost two this month' (p. 589). So children can be helped to identify the features of particular genre and to practise writing accordingly. We feel that the loud claims for direct instruction however, have been overstated.

Writing in subject areas

Writing throughout the school day and during each aspect of the curriculum is necessary for children to see that writing can be a tool for refining thinking about problems in biology or mathematics as well as telling stories. In addition, children who are expected to write in all areas of the curriculum can not be seen as passive learners dutifully memorising what the teacher has told them. Instead, they are active learners who have to think about what they are learning, reconstructing the concepts into their own language, because writing without thinking is impossible.

Winograd (1993) has given a detailed description of the writing that eight fifth-grade students undertake as they write original mathematics story problems. The classroom encouraged children to write their own mathematics problems in the form of stories and pose them to groups and the whole class for solving. Without any formal instruction in writing mathematical story problems, the students developed three strategies. The first strategy, used by the most mathematically proficient children in the classroom, was to use a focal, culminating question around which the writing was structured. This group of children monitored their writing by constantly asking themselves whether their writing was leading up to the focal question. The second strategy in common use was that of free association. In this strategy the culminating question was not identified until the writing was nearly complete. The third strategy was a combination of the previous two, but with the aim of increasing the difficulty of the problem. It was considered a status-enhancing move among the children to pose difficult problems.

Winograd's study is important because he demonstrates that children can use writing stories as a way of developing their mathematical understanding and also because the writing techniques the children use are similar to those in their everyday writing. Winograd's analysis of the first strategy fits in comfortably with the Flower and Hayes (1981) conceptualisation of the writing process discussed in Chapter 8.

Fortescue (1994) has described her experiences with her Grade 3 children's writing in mathematical journals. At the beginning of the year she was disappointed with the children's work because it was vague or not descriptive of the mathematics. She therefore introduced a series of instructional strategies, which involved not only talking about the mathematical content but also modelling how to talk and write about the activity by the teacher, as well as a system of checks and balances among the children, whereby their writing was read and commented upon by other children. Such a programme led to a marked improvement in her children's work. Fortescue considers that it is necessary to have group modelling and peer interaction before writing. But she has demonstrated that in her classroom:

'Through oral and written language, the children were not only able to complete the computation of multiplication problems, but they were also able to explain the processes that led them to the solutions.' (p. 579)

 **Summary**

Most of the writing we do as adults is non-fiction and yet many schools persist in providing opportunities for their students to write only personal narratives. There must be a wide range of topics for children to write about and a variety of teaching styles used to facilitate writing. While Freedman rightly sounds a note of caution about the deliberate teaching of genre, we suggest that there is much anecdotal evidence to suggest that children can and should practise writing widely in all areas of their curriculum. This recommendation is predicated on a curriculum which is interesting to the children, activity-based and where writing is seen as the responsibility of teachers in all subject areas and not confined to one part of the day labelled 'English', and taught only by English specialists.

What is the role of grammar?

CHAPTER 11

'Most of us speak or write conventionally, without being able to specify the rules.'
F. Smith, (1982) Writing and the Writer

For many years, the teaching of formal grammar was at the heart of the English curriculum. Generations of teachers have been trained to believe that children need to study and understand the grammar of their language before they can write well. In many countries and in many eras, newspaper editors, employers and university teachers regularly blame low levels of literacy on the 'deplorable' lack of understanding of grammar shown by school leavers. The debate over the proper role of grammar in assisting students' writing surfaces frequently in educational and non-educational circles alike, and has led to different policy emphases in different countries. In New Zealand, grammar has all but disappeared from the curriculum since the 1970s. Indeed, it was not examined in national school examinations after 1956 (E. Gordon, 1991). Yet, at the beginning of the century, it constituted more than 60% of New Zealand's school leaving examinations. Meanwhile, teachers in many other Western countries have continued to teach grammar, but with less conviction than their predecessors. In an American review, Hartwell (1985) commented that American textbooks and pedagogies continue to stress a mastery of formal grammar, 'but more and more researchers are questioning its benefits'.

What then, is the proper role of grammar teaching in learning to write? Is grammar important at all? How do children acquire their understanding of the grammar of their language? Should it be taught directly, or is it picked up incidentally? Does the correction of grammatical mistakes in children's writing help or hinder the process? These and other related issues are addressed in the pages that follow.

The case for direct grammar teaching

Throughout this chapter the word *grammar* refers to the systematic study of the rules underlying the formation of sentences. It refers to the study of the parts of speech (or form classes) such as nouns, verbs, adjectives, prepositions and the like. It refers to the study of different kinds of sentence patterns, clauses, phrases, subject and predicate. The assumption is that if students study the categories and structures that underlie their language, they will be able to use it more effectively. They will be able to discuss it intelligently, and avoid those misuses of the language which are typical of those students who have not studied grammar.

More specifically, the case for teaching grammar directly and regularly to all students, is as follows:

1 **Utilitarian argument.** The traditional case for teaching grammar is that it is useful for better writing and speaking. It helps students to see the logic of good writing, when, for example, there is a lack of agreement between subject and verb, when we say 'I' and not 'me', or when we have written an incomplete sentence. For instance, in the English textbook at the College of Education where one of the authors of this book trained as a teacher, the assertion was made that 'English grammar is indispensable... Its value is that it provides part of the technique for good writing' (I. Gordon, 1947). The average lay person in New Zealand probably supports this view, and Hartwell (1985) points out that popular discussions of the topic in the United States 'are almost unanimous in their call for a renewed emphasis on the teaching of formal grammar' (p. 106).

2 **Liberal education viewpoint.** Many educators argue that all students should understand the basis of the language they use every day. Language is a precious possession, unique to human beings, and a study of its logic and main features should be a vital part of everyone's education (Bauer, 1981).

3 **Foreign language learning.** Teachers of other languages claim that it is easier for students to study a foreign language if they know the structure of their own language. They become more aware of the differences between languages and can more readily predict when to change, and how to avoid interference from their own first language conventions. Students who cannot identify nouns and adjectives, for instance, are slower to realise and act on the fact that some languages place the adjective **after** the noun – unlike English.

4 **Terminology for teaching.** A fourth argument is that teachers need a common vocabulary to explain to students why their writing is 'incorrect' or 'inappropriate'. Teachers like to be able to show their students that it is undesirable stylistically to end sentences with a preposition; that the 'verb' should agree with its 'subject' in 'number'; that the 'pronouns' *I* and *we* are used for the 'subject' of a 'sentence', and so on. Generalising about such matters, and providing corrections and advice is so much easier if teacher and student share a common vocabulary.

5 **Other reasons.** There are no doubt other arguments advanced to justify the direct teaching of formal grammar in classrooms. Some believe, for instance, that students will **edit** their first written drafts more effectively if they know the rules of grammar; others believe that it will make our speech **more precise**; and many would assert that teachers need to know the structure of the language if they are to help their students use it more effectively – as individuals or in group teaching.

The case against traditional grammar

Each of these traditional arguments for grammar teaching can be challenged. While the last word has not been heard about some of them, we know more about their significance than we did fifty years ago when grammar was still the mainstay of the English curriculum.

1   **Utilitarian argument.** Common sense may support the view that a systematic study of grammar is helpful, yet several generations of researchers have repeatedly shown that it does not improve students' writing (see Hillocks, 1986; Elley et al., 1979). Other variables have shown a positive impact in the research, but grammar is not one of them. Studies of students at school often show low correlations between their grasp of grammar and their writing competence, and experimental studies show that grammar programmes are not as helpful as extra reading or writing, for instance. These studies are elaborated below, because many critics find their results counter-intuitive.

2   **Liberal education viewpoint.** While it may be desirable for all humans to know more about the basis of their language, this scarcely warrants the two hours per week for five or more school years that is traditionally devoted to grammar in many curricula. There are too many other interesting and more useful material for students to learn about language than repeated classification exercises can offer. Linguists may find fascination in the abstract study of grammar, but many students do not.

3   **Foreign language learning.** It is no doubt true that many students can master the grammar of a foreign language faster if they are familiar with common grammatical concepts of English. On the other hand, the time and effort taken by all students to reach the stage of development required of the few who learn a second language by means of a grammatical method, are harder to justify. There are more interesting and effective ways of acquiring a second language than the grammatical approach. Perhaps those who need this basic mastery can best learn it at the time it is required. Telling students that what they are learning now, with difficulty, in English lessons may be useful some day if they learn French or Japanese, is unlikely to convince many reluctant students. School curricula are already very crowded with new disciplines which students find more relevant to their interests and community needs.

4   **Terminology for teaching.** There may be validity in the rationale for providing teachers and pupils with a shared language for discussing common parts of speech. Students should be familiar with the labels for a few basic concepts – nouns, verbs, adjectives and the like. However, we have seldom found it helpful to try and explain to students why to use *he* and not *him*, or *does* and not *did* by resorting to rules about the object of a preposition, or agreement in tense between verb clauses, even amongst bright students who knew their grammar. Those most likely

to need such help are those least likely to understand such abstract explanations. At the point when we might introduce these technical labels, most pupils are not able to manipulate abstractions at all well. The rules which influence children's choice of words and structures are usually internalised in their first language, as a result of the imitation of significant language models in their environment – from parents, peers and teachers.

If correction of recurring grammatical faults is attempted, teachers will find it useful to provide models of the appropriate form for the students who need it, at the time they need it – when redrafting for publication, for instance. The research on regular correction of errors does not, in fact, support frequent correction (see p. 100).

5 **Other reasons.** Research on the benefits of grammar has not demonstrated any advantages for editing (as opposed to composing) as a result of a formal study of grammar. And if writing by students is unaffected by grammar study, it is even less likely that speech will be affected. There is just too little time to consider consciously the various options in the form of one's language production when one is in the full flight of conversation. The focus has to be on meaning, not form.

If these counter-arguments are accepted, there would seem to be little reason to teach formal grammar in the way that many primary and secondary teachers have traditionally done in many countries. However, we will not take the final step of recommending its abolition. There is a defensible case for teaching some grammar to some students, where it is judged to be needed. Teachers of English in particular will feel more confident in their teaching if they are able to see the consistencies in the language they teach and sometimes to explain them to others. English specialists should have a rich knowledge of their language, and those more curious students who genuinely want to know why the misrelated clause is ambiguous, could be told the grammatical explanation. Like other conventions, grammar is best taught, if at all, at the point of need. Many pupils cope very well without regular instruction in grammar, and many fluent writers are quite unable to analyse their own sentence structures as the grammar textbooks do.

 What does the research say?

The first systematic studies of the issues, early in the twentieth century, showed surprisingly low correlations between students' grammatical knowledge and their skill in writing (Rapeer, 1913). Indeed, these correlations were no higher than those between geographical knowledge and writing. These studies were soon followed by experimental studies to explore the relationship further. By 1963, at least ten such studies had been conducted (see Meckel, 1963) and although some lacked the rigour of more recent research, they consistently showed only negative findings on the benefits of grammar instruction. At that time, Braddock et al. (1963) in a parallel review, commented that grammar 'has a negligible... even harmful effect on the improvement in writing'. The reviewers were referring to the fact that time spent on grammar is time not spent on more productive activities for improving students' writing.

However, these studies were not enough to shake the faith of grammar supporters, as the research was frequently criticised for faults in design.

1 Most were too short in duration to show measurable benefits. It takes more than six months of study to have an impact on such a slowly developing ability as writing.

2 The studies were typically assessed by inadequate measures of language, such as an objective English test, or a single written essay.

3 They could not rule out the influence on the outcome of teachers' attitudes or competence, which can be crucial in small-scale studies.

These are legitimate criticisms, but even if the measures used were too unreliable, one would still expect that some of the studies conducted would favour the grammar instruction method. None did. The subjects who received grammar instruction methods were consistently worse off than those taught using the alternative methods. Clearly, the challenge to grammar teaching could not be ignored.

In the United Kingdom, a study by Harris (1962) clarified the situation further. It avoided many of the faults alleged to have existed in earlier studies as it involved as many as 228 students (aged 12–14 years) and five teachers; it continued for two years; used a variety of assessment criteria, and careful checks were made to ensure that the students studying grammar had in fact mastered enough grammatical concepts for these concepts to have a reasonable chance of influencing their writing. Five schools were involved, each teacher taught both a grammar and a non-grammar class, and the use of pretests in grammar and essay-writing allowed the researcher to clarify the outcomes. The non-grammar group spent more time reading and writing.

In spite of the fact that the grammar classes nearly doubled their pretest scores in grammar, by the end of the study they failed to show any advantage over the non-grammar groups in their writing ability, when judged on eleven objective criteria (essay length, number of common errors, sentence complexity, adjectival phrases, etc.). After nine months, the results were inconclusive. After two years however, the non-grammar groups were significantly better on 20% of the comparisons drawn, and the grammar groups were better in none. More specifically, the non-grammar students were writing more complex sentences with fewer errors.

Harris's study certainly weakened the argument for direct grammar teaching, but the critics still argued that the use of only one essay in the final post-test phase was insufficient. Moreover, the fact that the non-grammar group improved slightly in their knowledge of grammar suggested to some critics (Tomlinson, 1994) that Harris's comparison groups were not as pure as he had thought. Some uncertainty remained.

During the 1960s a number of new linguistic grammars emerged, and many teachers adopted them with high hopes. Bateman and Zidonis (1966) saw much merit in *Transformational Generative Grammar* (TG) which sets out to explain how we use surface structure (actual words) to express deep structures (what is understood), and the rules we use to transform one to the other. In a small-scale study of two classes they professed to show the TG-taught students produced more 'well formed' sentences than a control group. However, the study was flawed because the grammar students were academically brighter at the outset and because the differences in the teachers' attitudes and competence possibly favoured the TG group.

A review of several other such studies (Elley et al., 1979) showed that the promise of alternative grammars was no greater than that of traditional grammar.

Research since 1970

Between 1970 and 1973, a long-term study of the effects of traditional and TG grammar was conducted by Elley et al. (1975, 1979). Beginning with eight matched classes of 24 students (12- to 13-year-olds) in a large co-educational suburban secondary school, they designed an elaborate study in which the language development of these students was closely monitored over a period of three years. Each class followed one of three English courses – either TG grammar, traditional grammar or no grammar – for two periods a week, for three years. The non-grammar classes spent 40% of the extra time in English classes on free reading, 40% of the time on the study of set texts, and 20% on creative writing. They were not exposed to any grammatical terms. All other English activity (homework, etc.) was standardised. Each of the classes was taught by each of the three teacher-researchers for one of the three years in rotation (with minor exceptions) and each of the teachers expressed a genuine desire to see what would happen. They appeared neutral about the likely outcomes.

Throughout the three years, the students were assessed on a wide range of language tests – including at least 10 essays, on diverse topics – which were assessed using objective and subjective criteria, by independent and experienced examiners.

The results of this carefully controlled study were similar each year. Once again, no benefits were found to result from a regular study of either type of grammar. The students who learned no formal grammar for three years were writing just as fluently and 'correctly' as those who studied it for two periods a week over the three years. Small differences were noted in some of the objective tests, but they were all idiosyncratic, and probably due to chance effects. On the attitude scales the non-grammar group expressed the most positive attitudes towards English. After three years and 111 comparisons of mean scores, the authors concluded that:

'English grammar, whether traditional or transformational, has virtually no influence on the language development of typical secondary school students.'
(Elley et al., 1975, p. 38)

Moreover, no experimental study has appeared to contradict these findings in 90 years of research.

In a major review of 67 experimental studies designed to improve students' writing, Hillocks (1986) cited five recent studies of the grammar issue and found a negative impact overall (effect size -0.29). By contrast, studies of other approaches were generally positive; e.g., free writing studies (+0.16); inquiry methods (+0.57).

Furthermore, the picture is little different in other languages. A well-designed large-scale study of the issue in the Netherlands (Van de Gein, 1991) with nine-year-olds in six schools, confirmed these conclusions as far as the Dutch language is concerned. The researcher comments that even at the age of nine the students' prose is 'relatively autonomous'.

Not surprisingly, Hillocks concluded that 'nearly everything else is more effective in increasing the quality of writing' than time spent on a systematic study of English grammar.

Why is grammar so unhelpful?

It cannot be denied that, in the past, many teachers felt comfortable teaching formal English grammar. The content of grammar is clearly definable, neat, logical and progressive. It provides the teacher with something he/she knows, and the pupils do not. For instance, the teacher could introduce a lesson on adverbial clauses of manner, define them, illustrate them in sentences, set exercises requiring pupils to recognise them and then to modify them and create new examples. Next week they could be revised, then objectively tested – as either right or wrong. None of these fuzzy, subjective, debatable distinctions about appropriateness of style or infelicities of expression. Grammar was easy to teach, easy to test, and it used to be easy to defend. Of course it was helpful. Who would dream of questioning it?

Strangely, there have been many scholars of the past who did just that. Arlene Silberman (1991) points out that the great Renaissance scholar Erasmus had no patience with grammar teachers who wasted precious years hammering rules into children's heads. Montaigne believed his natural command of Latin, picked up from his tutor without rules, was destroyed by schoolmasters who insisted on rules. Rousseau and John Locke both argued against grammar. As far as we know, Plato never studied a Greek grammar, and Shakespeare never an English one. Considered then, from a long-term perspective, the burden of proof should have been placed on those who believe grammar study to be a useful way of spending pupils' time.

Why is grammar unhelpful? The research cited above has consistently shown that formal grammar, as a body of knowledge to be mastered, does not appear to transfer to students' writing. It does not say that students should ignore the rules/conventions of good English prose, and proceed to mix their tenses, ignore normal word sequence, and replace 'you' with 'youse'. These conventions are necessary to facilitate communication. The debate centres around the best way to learn them.

Throughout this book we have argued for teaching students at the point of need. Many students do learn most of the conventions themselves, from regular reading and practice at writing, from casual observation, and from informal discussion. Others, less fortunate, need more help. The research shows that special programmes which focus on the analysis of sentences are not helpful in generating new sentences. When students are composing, they apparently make use of autonomous language systems which they have internalised from their earliest verbal interactions with others. Extra time, then, spent on reading and writing, and observing others as they write, and discussing one's writing with teachers and peers is likely to be more productive.

What about correction of students' grammatical errors? Once again the research is consistent and counter-intuitive, at least for those teachers who have made a habit of such correction. For instance, studies by Shepherd (1992) with English students, by Semeke (1989) with German students studying English, and by Kepner (1991) with English students studying Spanish, all showed that those students whose errors were regularly corrected made no more improvement (usually less) than those whose writing errors were ignored and where the teachers commented on content. The message is reinforced by behavioural research studies (see Chapter 10) and research reviewed by Krashen (1994). Frank Smith, a long-time opponent of formal grammar teaching argues that 'emphasis on the suppression of errors results in the suppression of writing' (Smith, 1988, p. 30).

How do students learn their grammar?

Child development research shows that children internalise the conventions of grammar incidentally, through the many thousands of language events that take place in their lives from early childhood. Miller (1977) estimated that young children add new words to their vocabulary, incidentally and unconsciously, at a rate of one per hour while awake. In the same way, they learn the complexity of the grammar of their language – without formal instruction. They learn to sequence their words, adjectives before nouns, and subjects before predicates, long before they hear adults use these formal terms. They learn how to substitute pronouns for nouns, and how to form the past tense without being taught. We have all mastered and applied a multitude of implicit language rules, many of which linguists have failed to identify or describe. We can speak, write and understand sentences without being able to specify the rules by which they are produced.

How is it that we can all agree on the appropriate sequence of adjectives in a sentence such as the following – without knowing what the rules are for specifying that sequence?

'The three black South African breast-stroke swimmers arrived late.'

When did we learn that numerals precede adjectives of colour, which in turn precede adjectives of nationality, which in turn precede type of swimmer? These rules, like hundreds of others, are picked up incidentally, by engaging in real life verbal encounters, oral or written. When they are unknown they are best learned at the point of need, when students require them to express themselves, to communicate effectively, to reach a larger audience.

 ## Summary

The research cited above does not support the regular systematic teaching of formal grammar to students. However, we do not recommend that students never be exposed to the categories and rules of grammar. English teachers need it. Writers and editors and linguists like to discuss the finer points of sentence structure, and for them, the common terminology argument makes good sense. And for the majority of students, a brief introduction to the main rules which govern our sentence structures will be of interest. This is a different recommendation from allocating the study of grammar two hours per week for five or more years, and making its mastery a prerequisite for advancing in school or for selection for employment. We should realise that many good writers have learned to write effectively without an explicit knowledge of the subject.

12 Spelling

'Our sole purpose in teaching children to spell should be to enable them to write clearly, confidently and accurately.'

Croft, (1991)

How important is spelling?

Spelling, in the eyes of many people, is a crucial measure of a competent writer. Of course, it is important to use acceptable spelling for conveying our thoughts clearly to a wide range of readers. However, many university academics, business people, journalists and politicians have claimed that there is a decline in levels of literacy, largely on the basis of poor spelling. Indeed, quality of spelling has often been regarded as a barometer of the success of a school system. It doesn't seem to matter if pupils don't write, or if they write nonsense, as long as they spell what they **do** write, correctly. In perpetuating this attitude, critics are elevating spelling, which is essentially a tool, to a loftier position than it deserves in the hierarchy of educational values.

The fact is that the concept of a spelling 'error' hardly existed before the late eighteenth century. Before then, the spelling of a word was acceptable if it sounded right. In Shakespeare's time, his name was spelt in a dozen different ways. More recently, however, attitudes have hardened, and only one spelling is allowable. It is worth remembering that spelling is only a convention, and often an arbitrary one at that.

Why should spelling receive a disproportionate amount of attention from critics? Perhaps it is because with spelling there are no ambiguities. A word is either spelt correctly, or it is wrong. About that we can be dogmatic. And if we do not agree with what the writer is saying, and if we can also find a spelling mistake in his/her expression of it, then our suspicions that this person is sloppy and his/her thoughts are not to be trusted, are confirmed.

Spelling is a skill which is often tested but seldom systematically taught in school. Testing is not to be equated with teaching. Many of us can remember the weekly spelling test of 10 or 20 words on a Friday morning. The fortunate ones who spelled all words correctly received praise from the teacher while those who made mistakes were condemned to write out their corrections and exhorted to refrain from carelessness and to 'learn' their spelling. All too often, little guidance was given to students as to how to go about learning their spelling and few questioned the value of repeatedly writing out correct versions of misspelt words. Of course it is helpful, was the belief.

Is spelling important? Yes. Society expects the school to bring students to the stage where most words are spelt correctly. But the teacher who recognises that children are easily discouraged from writing by too great an emphasis on correct spelling will play down its importance at particular phases of their students' development. If they never write, they will never improve any aspects of their writing.

The English spelling system

Part of the difficulty many people experience with English spelling lies in the nature of written English. Unlike many other languages, English is not written phonetically. One symbol does not stand for one sound in English. We have approximately 44 sounds in English which have to be represented by 26 letters. Pitman and St John (1969) report that over 600 ways have been found to represent these 44 sounds. Some of the letters not only have different sounds, but often have no sound of their own. 'C', for instance, represents an 's' sound in 'ice' but has no sound of its own when it is written next to 'k' as in 'kick' or 'lick'. The picture becomes even more complicated in the case of vowels. One analysis showed that the five written vowels of English can be pronounced 48 different ways (Thorstad, 1991.) Think of the sounds represented by 'a' in 'ate', 'bat', 'bar', 'beautiful'.

But before we despair, let us note that there are advantages to having a language that has only an indirect relationship between its writing and its sounds. English is spelt the same way, regardless of the accent of the writer. An Australian pronounces 'dance' with a short 'a' sound, a New Zealander pronounces it with a long 'a' sound. But both write it in exactly the same way. Americans talk about 'tomatoes' where the 'a' is long (as in *mate*); New Zealanders pronounce the same word with an 'a' sound as in *mart*.

Spelling is neutral regarding dialect – we can hear differences between native speakers of American, Canadian and New Zealand English but these differences are not transmitted in writing. If English were a totally phonetic language we would require many more letters and diacritics (accent marks) which in turn would make reading more difficult for the many readers and speakers of the rich dialectal variations of English that are in existence today.

Of course, spelling is not totally arbitrary. It does have many links with the way words sound but it also has links with word meanings. As a general rule, words that sound the same but mean different things are spelt differently. Thus, we have 'vain' and 'vein,' 'horse' and 'hoarse,' or 'two' and 'too'. This distinction is very helpful for the reader as it acts as another cue to meaning, but is not so helpful for the writer who has to choose between alternative spellings.

Smith (1982) cites a delightful example of a sentence where all the words are spelt correctly, but when judged on meaning, the spellings are all totally wrong. The sentence is 'Wee eight sum meet four Ann our' (p. 150) which should be written as 'We ate some meat for an hour'. George Bernard Shaw pointed out the lack of phonetic regularity in English with the word 'ghoti,' which is pronounced 'fish' (*gh* as in enou**gh**, *o* as in w**o**men, and *ti* as in sta**ti**on).

The writing system benefits readers by providing letter-based cues to meaning, but this benefit is bought at the cost of extra effort on the part of the writer. While reading helps writing by providing the stimulus of fresh ideas, a wide vocabulary and different ways to structure writing, it may also mitigate against improved spelling because fluent readers do not read every letter in every word, or even every word. Fluent reading requires prediction and speed whereas producing a piece of prose requires letters to be written on the page (or typed on the keyboard) in a particular serial order. So spelling, in English, does require special effort on the part of most budding writers of the language. It comes as no surprise that there has always been a small percentage of children who have difficulty in learning to spell correctly. The best evidence available (e.g. Croft, 1983; Lamb, 1987) suggests that the standard of spelling has not changed in recent years in New Zealand.

How is spelling taught?

Class lists

One traditional approach has required children to memorise lists of words which are studied, used, and then tested on a regular basis. The word lists have been drawn from a range of sources. The most widely used lists in New Zealand schools, for many years, were those prepared by Schonell (1949). He grouped words into categories, according to common sounds or letter sequences, and pupils were required to learn a set of 10–20 words each week, whether they needed them or not. Whole class teaching was followed by whole class testing and individual differences were neglected.

Personal lists

A more recent approach requires students to make up personal spelling lists based on the words they need in their own writing in the classroom or outside. To help them produce such lists and spell the words they contain correctly, a number of word frequency lists have been prepared and published. These frequency lists are derived from an analysis of the words most commonly used in children's writing. For example, the New Zealand Council for Educational Research list of 2700 words, graded by frequency, was derived from an analysis of the writings of 6000 children (Arvidson, 1960; 1977). The Spell-Write list (Croft, 1983) lists 3200 words, based on the essays of 1250 New Zealand primary school pupils. In America, Rinsland (1945) graded more than six million words in 100 000 scripts of children from 416 American cities. Such surveys are intended to provide a core list which will meet the spelling needs of most pupils, most of the time. They are normally arranged in alphabetical order, and sometimes grouped by levels of frequency. Pupils keep them at hand during their writing, and use them to check the words they are unsure of, and to compile their own personal lists for learning later.

How effective are these contrasting approaches to spelling instruction?

Wilde (1990) summarises the traditional class list approach to teaching spelling as follows (p. 227):

> *'Although spelling programs differ in small ways and vary in quality, they are essentially alike in philosophy and format. Their primary goal is that students learn to spell a collection of words, typically 10-20 a week or 400-800 a year… The words to be learned are basically the same for all children, although textbooks may suggest that diagnostic pretests be used to assign some students to harder or easier books.'*

There are serious criticisms of this approach. First, it treats spelling as a separate curriculum area divided off from other aspects of a literacy curriculum. Many argue today that it should be taught as part of a writing programme (see Croft, 1983). Secondly, we know that most of the spelling errors pupils make are individual, peculiar to them alone (Croft, 1983). So a common list is unlikely to serve the needs of many pupils in a typical class. Thirdly, the traditional class list approach does not account for the vast number of words most adults can spell. Simple arithmetic shows that if a child learns 800 words a year during the time of formal spelling instruction, after six years he/she will have learned to spell only 4800 words, or only 2400 if we take the lower end of Wilde's figures. How then do we account for the many thousands of words that adults have correct spellings for? They can not all have been learned during formal spelling lessons. Indeed, there is some evidence that pupils who have no formal spelling lessons learn to spell just as well as those who do (Krashen, 1991; Courtis, 1949; Hammill et al., 1977). Manolakes (1975) showed that the average American pupil can correctly spell 75% of the words in the lists they will be called on to learn. Clearly, much spelling is 'caught' rather than 'taught'.

There is also little evidence to show that words learned to enable a child to pass Friday's test are retained for any length of time. Many are not well retained as they are not needed in the child's own writing. Nor is there evidence to show that words learned systematically from lists will necessarily be spelt correctly in the child's own writing later, when they are really needed. Many puzzled and frustrated teachers will reject this notion too.

In an effort to clarify the relative value of the two approaches, Freyberg (1964) set out to determine whether pupils learn better from class lists, such as those of Schonell or from personal lists prepared during writing sessions, using Arvidson's graded lists of 2700 words as a resource list. In 1960, all the Standard 3 (Year 5) pupils in a small New Zealand city were tested on a detailed word list and a short essay ('How I would spend £100'). All these pupils (n=760) had been taught by the Schonell class lists. Two years later, Freyberg repeated the survey on the 1962-cohort of Year 5 pupils, all of whom had been taught by the Arvidson method.

On the essay tests, the 1962-sample made significantly fewer errors.

Personal lists had certainly helped here. On the dictated word lists, however, there was no difference for better spellers, while the poorer spellers had a better performance if they studied the Schonell class lists. While the findings of Freyberg's study are not totally conclusive, they suggest that most pupils will benefit from preparing personal lists. Poor spellers may need extra systematic teaching of common words. After all, they have many more words to learn. However, it is better to delay direct teaching until it is clear that heavy-duty words are not being learned within the writing programme. Croft recommends that it not be done until age 9 or 10.

Learning the rules of spelling

Some textbooks suggest that spelling is best learned by memorising and applying spelling rules such as 'write i before e except after c'. Or, 'double the final consonant before adding *-ed* – if the verb has only one syllable'. The problem with this approach is that most rules are very complex and have many exceptions. Simon and Simon (cited in Peters, 1985) programmed a computer to spell by using over 200 spelling rules. When tested with 17 000 words the computer incorrectly spelled half the words. 'Coal', for example, was spelt 'cole', 'tie' was spelt 'ty' and 'bus' was spelt as 'buss'. If a computer cannot generate correct spelling by the logical application of a set of 200 rules, what chance do children have with a consciously learned set of such rules? This approach may provide a useful resource for some students, and assist them to gain insight into the spelling system. But most children will need much more than this.

How do we first learn to spell? A developmental viewpoint

The beginnings of spelling appear when children first attempt to write for themselves. Chapter 3 described how young children make letter-like scribbles on paper. Gradually these scribbles become refined to letter-like shapes and then to recognisable letters. A similar process goes on with spelling. Rough approximations to adult spellings become refined over time and with good teaching, develop into conventional spellings. Some people refer to children's first efforts at spelling by themselves as 'invented' or 'approximated' spelling.

We need to stress here that 'invented spelling' is not something that schools actually teach but rather a series of stages that children pass through on their path to becoming proficient spellers. Remnants of invented spelling strategies stay with us into adulthood. Whenever we guess at the spelling of a word we are unsure of, and fail to check it in the dictionary (and after all, often I can only find a word in a dictionary if I have a fair idea of how to spell it in the first place) or use our computer's spell checker, we are inventing a spelling. Invented spelling does have some real advantages. Clay (1987, p. 59) suggests that 'invented spelling can lead to a control over writing that frees the child to write the messages he wants to write'. When teachers deliberately provide the freedom to experiment with spelling, as well as with letter forms, they are giving the young child the freedom to write in his/her own way on a range of topics. Children's writing need not be confined to words which for which they already know the correct spelling. Once they are in full flight, they don't have to stop and ask the teacher for help, or ask their classmates or search wall dictionaries for the correct spelling. They merely make their best attempt, mark it in some way, and check it out later. The alternative to this freedom and desire to experiment is to restrict their writing to teacher-suggested topics, using words and word patterns supplied by the teacher. This situation is not so helpful if we want children to develop responsibility for their own improvement.

Gentry (1982) has examined the spelling of young children and shown that errors change over time in a systematic fashion as a result of the changing orthographic concepts the child develops. Drawing heavily on the work of Bissex, who documented her son Paul's progress from the age of 4 to 10, Gentry identified five stages young children go through on their way to becoming competent spellers (see Table 6). The stages Gentry identified are **precommunicative** (or deviant) where the child first uses symbols from the alphabet to represent words; **pre-phonetic** – a brief stage of only a few weeks in Paul's development, representing the first attempts at letter-sound correspondence.

Table 6 – *Spelling development (after Gentry, 1982)*

Stage	Characteristics	Examples
Deviant	Random ordering of letters, marks – often mixed with letters	bBp (=Monster) #PaH (=Giant)
Pre-phonetic	Two- and three-letter 'words' made up of speech sounds or letter names.	MsR (=Monster) DG (=Dog)
Phonetic	All sound features in the word represented by a symbol – as the child hears them.	PPL (=People) Chrobl (=Trouble)
Transitional	Vowels included in every syllable – some standard spelling and some phonetic.	Highcked (=Hiked) Tode (=Toad)
Standard (correct)	Mostly correct spelling.	People Hiked

Here Paul realised that letters have sounds and they can be used to represent sounds in words. Thus BRZ was written for 'birds', PKIHER for 'picture'. The pre-phonetic stage is followed by the **phonetic** stage where the writer tries to represent the entire sound structure in each word. Although the spellings do not necessarily represent conventional spelling for many words, the spellings are consistent. Thus PAULZ RABR SAF for 'Paul's robber safe.' This stage is marked by a conscious awareness that there is a consistency to spelling but that spellings can vary. Paul's mother notes that during this stage he commented that there were two spellings for cat, *K-A-T* or *C-A-T*. The fourth stage is a **transitional** stage where Paul no longer relied completely on a system of phonetic transcription. Instead, he began to place a greater reliance on visual and meaning-based ways of spelling words. An example is the spelling EIGHTEE for 'eighty'. Had Paul still been in the phonetic stage, this would have been spelt ATE. The final stage is labelled the **standard** (or correct) stage, where the writer has mastered the English orthographic system and its basic rules. Most words are now spelt correctly.

Gentry notes that changes from one stage to another are gradual and that spellings from two or more different stages may appear in the same piece of writing. He describes (p. 198) the growth in spelling as one in which

'children draw increasingly from alternative strategies – phonological, visual, and morphological. Development proceeds from simple to more complex, from concrete to more abstract form, towards differentiation and integration.'

The term 'invented spelling' has been used by detractors of current methods of literacy instruction, to imply that children are encouraged to make up their own spellings of words without any regard for conventional spellings. This is far from being the case. Invented spelling refers to the spellings young children use when they are beginning to write and reflect their understandings of the conventions of print. The 'inventions' children make are not random scribbles but have a consistency to them which reflects their imperfect understandings of English orthography. Because of some of the negative connotations that the term 'invented' has – that of making something up from scratch, many teachers prefer the term 'approximated' spelling as a more realistic representation of what children do when they are trying to spell a word. To deny children the opportunity to express their understandings of English, and insist that children spell everything they write with a conventional spelling will not only slow them down and inhibit their writing, as Clay (above) has suggested, but also deny the teacher an opportunity for diagnostic teaching. Careful analysis of the young child's errors, in the light of Gentry's description of stages, will help the teacher to target her teaching of spelling to the specific needs of individual children.

What do good spellers do?

In an interesting case study, Radebaugh (1985) examined the spelling strategies that 17 third- and fourth-grade students (in the USA) used. Nine of the students were classified as good spellers, while eight were considered poor spellers. The good spellers were found to break unknown or difficult words into parts (but not necessarily into syllables) and then try to write each part correctly. They also thought about the whole word, and tried to write it part by part; often they also tried to use spelling rules and thought about the 'hard spots'. Most importantly, they used visual imagery. For example, one child visualised the word 'arithmetic' on her textbook, while two others used a memory of the appearance of a road sign to help them spell 'cautiously'. By contrast, the poorer spellers were able to describe only a few strategies and they depended on letter-by-letter phonetic strategies. Poor spellers made no reference to visual images.

In another small-scale case study, Weiner (1994) had four first graders (two of whom were considered good spellers, and two poor spellers) verbalise to a puppet what they did as they spelled. The results were interpreted to show that there was a clear progression from phonetic spelling to an understanding of word patterns. What was interesting were the explanations the children offered about their strategies. The poor spellers relied on letter/sound knowledge and explained that this was what they were doing. The good spellers did not appear to rely as much on letter/sound associations, but actually said that they did. It would appear that the good spellers had acquired a number of techniques (such as a knowledge of what the words looked like and more risk-taking in their writing) but were unaware that they were using these techniques. While the findings of these studies are limited by the small number of subjects, they are important because the researchers tried to discover from the children their understanding of what they are doing when they spell.

In a larger New Zealand study of 200 Form 1 (Year 7) students, DeAth (1984) showed that good spellers paid close attention to print. They proof-read better, made fewer miscues, and pronounced artificial words better in contrived reading passages, than did poor spellers matched by age and general ability. When questioned about their learning strategies, good spellers also showed greater self-discipline. They identified 'hard spots' in words, exaggerated the pronunciation of tricky words (Feb**ru**ary, Wed**ne**sday), and often indulged in trial writing – 'to see if it looked right'. The key role of visual attention to letter sequences was clear in this research. DeAth concluded that pupils should be allowed time in their language programme to focus on the **form** of the words they use. Similar recommendations came from comparable research by Radebaugh (1985) cited above, and Roberts and Ehri (1983). Again, we can emphasise that this is best done in the context of ongoing writing.

How do we learn to spell new words?

The research cited above seems to indicate that we best learn to spell words as we need them in our writing. Spelling is no different from other forms of learning in that purpose and motivation are all-important. The bulk of research supports the view that visual memory is involved but there is more to spelling than rote memory. Putting the word in memory is usually not the main problem. Accessing the word from that memory and selecting the correct word from a range of alternatives are more difficult. Thus the criterion for our choice of words for spelling acquisition should be the theme or topic we are writing about in the classroom. There is little point in trying to learn to spell words that we will never use in our daily writing. Many children are very good at short term retention, where words are remembered long enough to pass a test and then forgotten. School days are too short to waste time in pointless memorising of words we will not use in our writing. Thus, for most pupils, this chapter rejects spelling programmes based on lists or spelling textbooks that use words that are not derived from the children's own writing.

The starting point to a successful spelling programme is a rich writing environment where the children are writing about a range of topics, using a range of genres, and writing because they have something they want other people to read. An environment that is rich in print is needed for children to master the intricacies of English spelling. Wilde (1990) advocates wide reading and a process approach to writing, as well as instructing children on effective strategies for learning spelling.

Extensive reading is important in learning to spell in as much as children can be encouraged to look at words that they do not understand or that are new to them. This particularly applies to non-fiction writing where specialised vocabulary is often met for the first time. Word study skills, where children examine and discuss the similarities and differences between words, at the level of both letter forms and meaning, are worthy of attention at some time during the classroom day. But we rarely advocate teaching word study skills in isolation. These activities should rather be incorporated into the context of purposeful reading and writing.

A very important part of developing a spelling programme is to teach children how to learn to spell difficult or new words they will need. The desired goal of all spelling programmes should be that children be able to automatically access the orthographic form of the words they need when they need them. This access is translated smoothly into the motor skill of putting down, one after another, the correct sequence of letters.

Thus it is helpful if children understand that spelling is a visual-motor skill requiring them to recall from their memory banks the acceptable spelling of a word. So to learn the spelling of words efficiently, both visual and motor processes should be used. The child needs to look at the target word intently, observing the sound, letter patterns and meaning relationships of the word, and then copy it out correctly. Thus, the 'look and feel' of the word is imprinted on the child's mind. Peters (1985) suggests that vocalisation at the same time as copying or writing the word will help in this process, but it is important that the vocalisation be concurrent with writing the word as a whole.

There is a body of research which shows that a specific spelling-learning system can be very effective if it is made habitual. In a series of studies with poor spellers, Church (1990) has shown that the rehearsal training system recommended by Croft (1983), accompanied by daily feedback, leads to impressive gains in the spelling of new words. Croft's system, detailed in the New Zealand 'Spell-Write' programme, requires students to:

1 Copy the word.

2 Check it.

3 Study it 'look, note shape, say it, hear its sound'.

4 Learn it 'say it again, spell the letters, write it'.

5 Test yourself.

6 Check it.

In the first such study, McBreen-Kerr, reported in Church (1990), tutored a 13-year-old boy who was having difficulty with spelling. Each day, five new words were studied, all of which had been misspelt. After checking baseline levels, the boy was trained using the Croft method and in the course of daily sessions, improved from 1.7 words correct (out of 5.0) to an average of 4.0 words correct per day. Similar results have been reported in seven parallel studies. Such findings are good news for those students with chronic spelling problems. Many of them need to establish a system like Croft's, and to apply it regularly.

Another part of any good spelling programme is teaching children proof-reading skills, and showing them how to detect and correct their own spelling errors. Included in this would be strategies for finding words in various sources – dictionaries, wall charts, special lists, and other children's writing. We need to remember that fluent reading often works against careful proof-reading, because the reader (if he/she has been the writer) has a strong expectation of seeing what they think they wrote, instead of what was actually written. One effective method of proof-reading requires children to work in pairs where each child checks the other's writing.

It is widely recommended that consistent misspellings should be rewritten correctly in a personal notebook for later study (see Croft, 1983). With this system, the learners determine which words they consider necessary to learn, and build up their own lists. Instruction about how best to learn words, as well as an allotment of time, must also be provided for children to learn their personal lists. Too often this is a task relegated to homework which in turn is dependent, for its accomplishment, on the vagaries of sufficient quiet time and interested parents or siblings. Similarly, teachers may assume that their children possess the necessary meta-cognitive skills to allow them to learn words. Unfortunately, this is not always so, and many children need to be given good demonstrations of learning-systems such as those outlined above. Teacher modelling has a key role to play here too.

Persistent errors should be analysed so that diagnostic teaching is used to remedy the errors. Is the error with the vowels? Are the words spelt phonetically? Has the child made a semantic confusion with 'there' and 'their'? We should be long past the days when our only response to spelling errors was to mark them as wrong and then expect the child to correct them and memorise the appropriate spelling.

Bartch (1992) has written in detail about a spelling programme that uses many of the ideas discussed above. Dissatisfied with a traditional spelling list programme in which the same children excelled week after week, and the same children always failed, she adopted a procedure whereby children built up their own banks of words to learn, drawn from their own writing. Formal weekly tests were replaced with a weekly 45-minute 'strategy' time that involved 'mini-lessons' on topics such as constructing a word bank, using a dictionary or thesaurus, experimenting with spelling, word study and finding and correcting errors. Bartch uses anecdotal evidence as proof of the success of her programme. Parents of the children in her class were supportive of the methods she was using and reported that they noticed a more positive attitude in their children towards spelling. As children write, Bartch comments that

'…they use their strategies for spelling their words. I find that they refer to their spelling boxes, word wall, book resources, and even help each other with spellings. During shared reading, children often notice words with special endings in the big books. We often stop to talk about language. They are much more aware of the English language as a result of the new approach. There is a new awareness on the part of the children concerning words and relationships among words.' (p. 407)

 ## Spell checkers and computers – a cautionary note

In spite of predictions from computer enthusiasts, spelling is still a human function and can only be assisted by a computer. Computer spell checkers take no account of meaning – if a misspelt word is a legitimate word, it will not be corrected. For instance, typographic slips such as 'tow' for 'two' or 'there' for 'their' will go unmarked by the computer. When an error is detected, the computer will present the writer with a list of words. The appropriate word has then to be selected by the writer. So spelling remains a human function of writing, involving choice and decision making based upon linguistic knowledge, not all of which can be replaced by an electronic device.

 ## Summary

Learning to spell requires an understanding not only of the sound system of English but also of the relationship between letters and meanings. Spelling is more than just a mechanical process dependent only on rote memory. Young children's progress in spelling goes through clearly definable stages dependent on their growing understanding of the links between orthography and sounds.

We advocate a multi-pronged approach to spelling instruction. First, all children should be expected to learn a basic core of 300 or so high-frequency words (see Croft, 1983). Secondly, new or troublesome words derived from the children's own writing and current classroom themes should be recorded in a personal list. Thirdly, meta-cognitive strategies for learning correct spellings, such as those recommended by Croft, need to be demonstrated and practised with children. Fourthly, children should be shown strategies for tackling the spelling of new words – such as hard-spotting, visualising, spelling by analogy with known words, and dictionary checking. They should also be taught a few basic spelling rules which are of wide application. Fifthly, children should be encouraged to take responsibility for their own spelling improvement, and to develop a spelling conscience. But above all else, the classroom should be a place filled with purposeful reading and writing so that teachers can frequently draw pupils' attention to the form of new words and children can teach themselves when they see a real need.

13 Technologies and writing

'Although much has changed in the world of written language since that first mark on a stone or clay slab, although complex machines have replaced simple tools... the fundamental nature of written language has remained constant.'

A. Purves, (1990) The Scribal Society

What is the role of computers in teaching children to write? Are they helpful? Will they become essential? Will they take over? Will they change the way we look at the importance of literacy?

Computers are now an accepted part of our world. Almost everybody uses one in some form or other in their daily life. Withdrawing money from a money machine, making a booking to travel, requesting a telephone number from directory service, all involve using some form of computer. Almost everything we read now has been processed by a computer at some stage of its development. Many homes have personal computers. By September 1995, there was a personal computer in 25% of American homes; the corresponding figure for New Zealand homes is 21%. Most schools also have computers in their classrooms. While the ratio in New Zealand schools in the mid 1990s is one computer to 17 students, by the end of the century this ratio is expected to improve to one computer for every five students.

What are all these computers used for? Surveys show that the most frequent use of computers in primary schools is for word processing. In other words, children are using computers for writing. As we will point out, computers are already having an effect on how we write and what we write.

In this chapter we propose to review historical changes in the technology of writing, and show that the computer can be seen as another stage in the development of writing technology. For just as a pencil and exercise book are forms of technology used for writing, so too the computer can be seen as an expensive example of such technology.

A little history

Writing itself is a technology. A writer needs something to write on and something to write with. Technologies used for writing in school over the last 100 years have changed drastically. One hundred years ago children wrote on slates with chalk. This had the advantage of being relatively cheap and requiring little maintenance apart from a periodic repainting of the surfaces the chalk was used on. The main disadvantage was that the writing was not permanent – it was erased, and so one of writing's prime functions

– that of establishing a permanent record – was not fulfilled.

In the 1930s slates and chalk were gradually superseded by pencils and paper. The advantage of this technology was that, like slates and chalk, it was cheap. Pencils and paper also had the advantage of permanence but at the same time mistakes could be erased and rewritten. Drawbacks were few – pencils broke and needed resharpening. Pencil and paper still form many children's introduction to writing today.

As children progressed through the school system, pencils were replaced by pen and ink. In the 1940s, dip pens with steel nibs were used; they were soon replaced by fountain-pens as these became cheaper. Difficulties with these technologies were few. Pen and ink were relatively cheap. However, in the hands of the less meticulous pupil, ink could be messy and corrections or changes in the text were difficult to make. For children who wrote with their left hand, smudging was inevitable. Attempts to make left-handed children write with their right hand often coincided with the switch from writing with pencils to writing with pens. Such attempts often gave rise to conflict and controversy about the consequences for the left-handers' mental health.

The ball-point pen was invented in 1938, although its refined version with a ball that rolled freely was not available until the early sixties. Then it rapidly replaced the fountain-pen as the writing technology of choice.

Each of these novel technologies has been introduced to schools only after a lengthy debate. Ball-point pens, for example, were banned by many schools for some time after their acceptance in the world beyond the classroom. Traditionalists felt that ball-point pens would encourage sloppy handwriting and that the finished writing was not as aesthetically pleasing as work written in pen and ink. Perhaps there was also a lingering puritanism which felt that anything that made writing easier was not to be encouraged. However, the improved ink-flow, convenience and cheapness eventually saw the technology of the ball-point pen replace the fountain-pen.

Typewriters made relatively little impact on writing in schools. In the junior classes their use was usually confined to a play object and in secondary schools for girls to learn to use in specific classes as a form of vocational training. Apart from cost, it is difficult to understand why typewriters had so little effect. The reason is possibly that the mechanical aspects were not sufficiently refined – keyboards were inflexible, ribbons were messy to replace and the machines broke down frequently. More seriously, typed work was difficult to revise, and revision is a necessary component in quality writing. Gender stereotyping may have played a part too, as typewriters were almost universally used in the work-place by women and the occupation of secretary was not seen as a high status position.

While each of these technologies – slates, pencils, pen and ink, ball-point pens and typewriters – has influenced writing to some extent, none has had the dramatic effect of computers which have the power to change not only the appearance of printed material, but also the nature of writing itself.

Word processing research

Research on the use of computers in schools can be divided into two areas – research on the effects of word processing on pupils' writing, and speculative research into conceptual changes computers may cause.

Many schools use computers for word processing as an intelligent typewriter which is capable of producing a story which looks just like a printed story in a book. To achieve this effect, the story has to be composed, keyed into the computer, checked for accuracy, and finally printed out. The computer is used as a way of producing a perfect final copy. Some classrooms enlist the help of parents to type directly into the computer what the children have already written. Increasingly however, children are composing their material at the keyboard and putting it directly into the computer themselves.

Numerous researchers have surveyed the rapidly expanding literature on computers as word processors in classrooms. A comprehensive review was carried out by Cochrane-Smith (1991). She argues that the introduction of a new technology is influenced by and influences the social nature of the classroom.

'How word processing works in elementary classrooms is partly a function of how individual teachers work. How word processing affects children's writing practices is partly a result of the way these are socially organised.' (p. 117)

While many research studies show that children revise more frequently when using a word processor, Cochrane-Smith was critical of the significance of this finding. She argued that many of the revisions made are trivial and that the number of revisions is not necessarily an indicator of quality. A similar interpretation could be made from research studies that show children produce a greater quantity of writing when using a word processor. She considered that definitive conclusions about the effects of word processing on quality of writing were simply not yet possible at that time (1991). However, she did concede that the use of word processing allows children to produce texts with fewer errors and that are more attractive to read. Perhaps there is a differential effect on children, depending on the age of the child. Indeed, the literature has tended to focus on the effect of word processing on college and high school students and neglected to study younger children.

Bangert-Drowns (1993) subsequently carried out a meta-analysis of 32 experimental studies that compared two groups of students where both groups were receiving identical instruction, but only one group was using computers as word processors. His overall conclusions were that using a word processor did help younger students and weaker students improve the quality of their writing, and that students using a word processor produced a greater quantity of material than students in the contrast groups. In spite of improved quality and quantity of writing, however, use of a word processor did not appear to engender a more positive attitude to writing. Bangert-Drowns commented that the findings from such studies of word processing have been ambiguous and, like Cochrane-Smith, he suggested that the effect appears to be influenced by the classroom context.

One of the largest and longest running projects which examined the effects of using the computer as a tool for writing is that of the QUILL project. Bruce and Rubin (1993) began their project in 1981, introducing the QUILL program throughout the USA and particularly in Alaska, where there are a large number of small schools in widely scattered communities. The computer program (which does not require a sophisticated computer to run), consists of a Planner, a Library and a Mailbag. The Planner allows students to organise their ideas for writing. This is where the students do most of their writing. The Library allows students to store their writing and allows others access to read it. Mailbag is a message system that allows children to send messages to other children, or their teacher, and also acts as a bulletin-board.

Summative evaluation showed that for specified types of writing, students in classrooms using QUILL improved their writing skills more than students in classrooms which did not use the programme. More importantly, in Bruce and Rubin's eyes, are the qualitative changes that are associated with the introduction of the QUILL programme. These include changes to the manner and frequency of communications between children and between teachers as well as between teachers and children. A new technology for writing was shown to bring about changes, many unanticipated, that reach beyond the school's writing curriculum. The researchers also suggested that changes caused by the introduction of new technology may be gradual, and may continue long after the evaluation project has finished.

Snyder (1993) also surveyed the literature relating to word processing from a different angle. She examined the opinions of professional writers, and anecdotal reports from teachers and research studies. Professional writers varied in their enthusiasm for using computers. Some, such as Len Deighton (a writer of thrillers) and Douglas Adams (a science fiction writer) were extremely enthusiastic. Others, such as Iris Murdoch (an English novelist) avoided using any form of computer technology in their writing.

Anecdotal reports from teachers were generally enthusiastic. Teachers claimed that students are writing more, and revising more, with computers. Some teachers felt that the introduction of word processors does little to improve the quality of children's writing unless they are used in conjunction with an effective teacher and a worthwhile writing programme. An analysis of 57 research studies led Snyder to conclude (p. 63) that:

> *'Most writers, regardless of age, enjoy writing with word processors, and believe that their use enhances composing and revising strategies, as well as the quality of their writing. The texts produced have fewer errors than those written with pens, and many students write longer texts with word processors than with traditional tools. Students tend to revise more but at a surface level rather than at a meaning level. The findings in regard to quality are more equivocal. However, more studies have found an improvement in quality.'*

These comprehensive reviews of a recent but voluminous literature suggest that the social context of the classroom and the pedagogy used by the school in respect of writing will be more influential in children's writing than the mere adoption of this technology. However, the findings are certainly promising, if not as dramatic as the first enthusiasts were claiming.

Looked at logically, word processing should take some of the drudgery out of writing for children. No longer do children have to carefully form letters on a page – the computer takes care of that as well as of the complete layout on the page. At the editing stage, spelling checkers enable the writer to proof-read the document. They can provide a child with a required word without provoking the all-too-often pious cry from the teacher 'Have you looked it up?'. Although the spelling checker that will decide whether the author intended 'tow' or 'two' has not yet been developed, grammar checkers can assist in making the correction. A built-in thesaurus can help provide that elusive word, or vary one's own word choice. Machines offer help without judgement or comment. Some programmes can produce borders to go around the page; different fonts can be selected at the stroke of a key while some programmes allow the writer to illustrate the work with drawings.

Offsetting these advantages of word processors are the difficulty of typing material in and the cost and accessibility of the machines. A perennial challenge for writers is that most of us think much faster than we can physically put the words down on paper. If typing proceeds only by means of two fingers with lengthy searches for the next letter, then the gap between mental rehearsal and setting down the ideas is further widened.

Nevertheless, the mechanical skill of typing is no more difficult than playing a musical instrument. A six- or seven-year-old who can play the piano or the recorder is not considered a prodigy. If word processors are to be used more widely in schools, then we should teach all children to touch-type. Meanwhile, voice recognition software is being developed and if it ever becomes affordable and universal, it may further change the nature of writing.

Accessibility is also a problem. Computers suitable for word processing are still expensive – a vast number of exercise books and pens can be bought for the cost of one computer. Then there are the hidden costs of maintenance, software purchases and a never-ending stream of upgraded programmes which must be bought. While a few of the more elite private schools may require all children to have their own laptop computer, most classrooms in primary schools have only one or two computers available in each classroom for children to use. If the physical act of writing is inseparable from composing then we are still a long way from allowing all children to take advantage of a word processor.

Future trends

As computer technology becomes commonplace in schools, we can expect it to influence not only the way we write but also the form of what is written.

According to Bolter (1991, p. 3):

> *'The computer is restructuring our current economy of writing. It is changing the cultural status of writing as well as the method of producing books. It is changing the relationship of the author to the text and of both author and text to the reader.'*

Several examples illustrate these points.

Input devices

Today the chief means of putting information into a computer is by typing at a keyboard. Voice recognition programmes are being developed which will allow a writer to dictate directly into the computer. If the historical trends of computer software development continue, these programmes will rapidly become more effective and cheaper. The labour of typing will be abolished. Such a change will also affect what is written. Elsewhere we have discussed the relationship between speech and writing. If voice processing software is widely used can we expect the printed word to become more like the spoken word – that is, less concise, less formal, and more repetitive? (See Chapter 2.)

Computer technology also allows the easy copying of information from one document to another. Thus a child writing a report on spiders can look up the encyclopedia on CD-ROM and automatically copy the relevant parts into the report – with acknowledgement, of course. Or, alternatively, a search can be made on the Internet and the relevant material copied into the document. So a report can directly use material from a range of sources without laborious rewriting. In turn, widespread use of these technologies may mean that society will have to rethink questions of ownership of intellectual property and redefine the boundaries between legitimate use of published work and plagiarism.

Hypertext

Hypertext is another major innovation that computers bring to writing. Hypertext allows prose to be layered – a word or phrase can be marked, and when the appropriate key is pushed, the phrase will be explained and expounded. In turn, the explanation itself can be further detailed. This means that the writer, instead of having one layer of prose in which to write, has the challenge of multiple levels. Each layer can be tailored to the differing needs of readers. For example, a recipe written in hypertext may have at its first level the recipe written for an experienced cook. The recipe may list as an ingredient self-raising flour and in its method suggest creaming the butter and sugar. A novice cook who may not know what self-raising flour is, can click on flour and be told exactly what it is. Similarly, the novice can click on 'cream the butter and sugar' and be told how to mix the butter and sugar together. The flexibility of computers may allow the writer to include pictures and even video clips to illustrate aspects of the writing. A rough analogy to hypertext is the use of explanatory footnotes by some non-fiction writers, but in hypertext the footnotes can be accessed immediately by the reader instead of making the reader turn the page repeatedly or look at the end of the chapter. In other words, the linear way that the reader reads and the writer writes may no longer be appropriate. Bolter (1991) suggests that we may be returning to a writing and layout style similar to that of the Middle Ages when medieval texts were annotated in the margins and also contained numerous illustrations.

Electronic communication

The power of the computer to allow rapid and relatively easy editing means that collaborative writing is also easier. The range of collaborative writing can also be extended. Many schools are now connected to the Internet which means that writing partners can be situated in another school, another town or even another country. E-mail allows instantaneous and cheap written communication between people. The past two decades have seen a decline in letter writing as telephone long-distance calls became cheaper. This trend may be reversed by e-mail which is less expensive and almost as immediate as a telephone conversation. Programmes are now available for interactive dialogues via e-mail. The only difference is that the communication is written rather than spoken. Again, these technologies may alter the nature of writing. Where letters were seen as deliberate, planned communication which could also serve as a permanent record, e-mail can be rapid and spontaneous, and unless a paper copy is printed by the receiver, ephemeral.

E-mail is developing its own conventions. Writing in capital letters is a way of expressing extreme outrage, bordering on rudeness. There are also conventions to signal jokes (always a problem when writing for an unseen audience).

Internet facilities mean that, as well as being able to access information on a global scale, writers can publish their writings on a global scale. There is no need to go through the cumbersome procedure of printing on paper, binding and distributing the products of our writing. Several keystrokes will allow material to be 'published' on the Internet and to become accessible to anyone else connected to the Internet.

Increasing cognitive skills

The improvements that computers will make in writing as described above are insignificant when compared with the claims some educators make for computers. Scardamalia and her colleagues in Toronto (1994) claim that the benefits of implementing CSILE (Computer Supported Intentional Learning Environment) will dramatically enhance children's cognitive skills. CSILE consists of a database which all students can access. Use of the database means that knowledge becomes communally constructed and is more powerful than knowledge which exists only in the minds of individuals. Students communicate through text and graphics; they add their own comments and illustrations to the work of their peers. They read, write, and critique the writing of their classmates. Scardamalia claims that learning, rather than completing tasks for the teacher, is the outcome of the

CSILE project. Writing onto a shared database is the tool but learning is the outcome. Scardamalia draws on both Vygotsky's social-construction theory of knowledge as well as Popper's theory of knowledge (where knowledge resides in institutions as well as individuals) as a framework for CSILE. The researchers present data from objective achievement tests as well as anecdotal evidence to support their contentions.

 ## Summary

Computing technology is not only changing the way we write but it also influences what we write about and even perhaps the way we think. Scardamalia et al. (1994) make sweeping claims for computer assisted writing via a publicly accessible data base as a way of enhancing cognitive skills.

While there is evidence that children write more, with greater ease and fewer errors, and that publishing is simpler with modern technology, we should not become so blinded by the technology that we overlook the vital role that effective teaching will play in a modern classroom. Machines can strengthen good teaching, but they are no substitute for it.

CHAPTER **14**   # Developmental descriptions of children's writing

'I doubt whether there is a fixed sequence through which all children must pass. The path to progress is likely to be different for different children.'

M. Clay, (1987) *Writing Begins at Home*

How can we best describe the phases of children's development?

Since the late 1980s and in the 1990s, educators in the western world have attempted to spell out, in more detail than was previously the case, the various indicators of children's development which show what stage each child has reached. The assumption is that most students pass through similar lines of development in various aspects of the curriculum, and that teachers who understand the milestones and indicators of each phase or level will be better able to guide their students with advice and help appropriate for their level.

Debate continues about the validity of these assumptions in language areas, and about the best way to describe the phases, and even how many might usefully be described. For instance, in the case of early writing, New Zealand publications have typically spelled out three overlapping stages – **Emergent**, **Early** and **Fluent**. (See, for instance, *Dancing with the Pen* (Ministry of Education, 1992) and Eggleton & Windsor (1995).) Table 7 lists the targets children are to aim at in these three levels in the Eggleton & Windsor model. Another scheme, widely used in New Zealand and Australia, is that of the Western Australian Education Department, The *Writing Developmental Continuum*, which describes indicators for six phases, as follows:-

1   Role play writing

2   Experimental writing

3   Early writing

4   Conventional writing

5   Proficient writing

6   Advanced writing.

In the 'standards' movement in Britain, educators attempted to define ten levels of development in each area of the national curriculum. In the 1993 Revisions, the National Curriculum Council listed these standards for writing:

Table 7 – *Children's targets in early writing, classified by level and process/product*
       Adapted from Eggleton and Windsor (1995, pp. 13–17)

	Emergent level	Early level	Fluent level
Process-Focus	To have correct directional movement To leave spaces between words To use approximations according to the sounds heard at the beginnings of words To begin to use some high-frequency words	To use beginning and end sounds of words To use vowels To spell many high-frequency words correctly To use more correctly spelt words than approximations To begin using editing skills – to place fullstops – to place capitals – to locate approximations by underlining To begin to correct approximations by using word sources	To use editing skills – thinking about the message of writing – using most punctuation marks correctly – dividing written work into paragraphs – recording and presenting information in different ways – using a dictionary and thesaurus
Product-Focus	To be able to choose a topic to write on To use own experiences for writing To begin to talk about some features of own writing To be able to present a piece of writing for others to share.	To understand that words carry many kinds of information To know that writing must make sense To be able to select from a wide range of topics and genre To be able to choose an appropriate title To begin to make some corrections to meaning To begin to realise that writing can involve a number of stages To begin to record and present information in different ways	To use variety in sentence beginnings To sequence ideas To use an increasingly wide vocabulary To write spontaneously to record personal experiences (expressive) To write descriptively on a variety of topics, shaping ideas and experimenting with language and form To write instructions and recount events in authentic contexts (transactional) To begin to explore choices made by writers and apply to own writing

At level 1, for instance, students were expected to hold a pencil correctly, to write their own names and something about themselves, and to discriminate between letters and words.

At level 3, sample standards specified that students should be able to produce simple, complete pieces of fiction or non-fiction, which convey meaning clearly, with proper agreement of subject and verb, and to use capital letters, full stops and question marks correctly.

For level 5, students were expected to write coherent sentences, using paragraphing, wide vocabulary, complex structures, apostrophes and speech marks.

These developmental schemes may vary also in the breadth of their aims

– some focusing merely on a few products and processes, some listing key features of text and inferred underlying understandings while some describe phases in spelling, handwriting, grammar and writer's strategies.

The New Zealand curriculum classifies writing into three functions – **Expressive**, **Poetic** and **Transactional**, with eight cumulative levels in each (see Table 8). The vagueness of the achievement objectives found in each level demonstrates the difficulty that the authors had in differentiating between them. It can be argued that the aims of writing are very similar at each stage from six to sixteen years – varying mainly in the range of topics written about, the breadth of vocabulary used, the variety of sentence structures and the greater mastery over conventions such as punctuation and spelling.

Nevertheless there are enough differences which can be detected by astute observations, particularly in the early phases, to make the exercise seem worthwhile. With the aid of exemplars of student writing at each stage, it is possible to sensitise teachers to the various signs of progress, and assist them with formative assessment, and with ideas for more judicious teaching, suited to their students' needs. However, we caution readers to realise that the descriptions of each phase are often general rather than specific, that the phases do overlap, and that some students do not follow the orthodox sequence. Children may show several of the indicators of one phase, but simultaneously other indicators of phases above and below.

As the West Australian scheme is unlikely to be as widely known as the New Zealand Curriculum, and as it spells out a greater variety of specific indicators, and is consistent with many of the features of this book, it is used below to illustrate how a knowledge of the various phases could enrich teachers' understanding of their students' growth. For further details, see the original publication *Writing Developmental Continuum* (1994).

Specimen Indicators from the Western Australian Developmental Scheme (adapted)

We have also included some examples of children's writing to illustrate these indicators.

Phase 1: Role play writing

At this phase, children are experimenting with marks on paper, mixing together approximations of letters, numbers and other symbols. Five types (out of more than 30) of indicators of phase one are:

Ben's biscuit: phase 1 writing

the writer

- assigns a message to his or her own symbols
- understands that drawing and writing are different
- places letters randomly on a page
- shows beginning awareness of directionality
- attempts to write his/her own name.

Table 8 – *Levels of the New Zealand Curriculum – Written language: achievement objectives*

Writing functions

	Expressive writing	Poetic writing	Transactional writing
Level 1	Students should: • write spontaneously to record personal experiences	Students should: • write on a variety of topics, beginning to shape ideas	Students should: • write instructions and recount events in authentic contexts
Level 2	• write regularly and spontaneously to record personal experiences and observations	• write on a variety of topics, shaping ideas in a number of genres, such as letters, poems, and narrative, and making choices in language and form	• write instructions and explanations, state facts and opinions, and recount events in a range of authentic contexts
Level 3	• write regularly and with ease to express personal responses to different experiences and to record observations and ideas	• write on a variety of topics, shaping, editing, and reworking texts in a range of genres, and using vocabulary and conventions, such as spelling and sentence structure, appropriate to the genre	• write instructions, explanations, and factual accounts, and express personal viewpoints, in a range of authentic contexts, sequencing ideas logically
Level 4	• write regularly and with ease to express personal responses to a range of experiences and texts, explore ideas, and record observations	• write on a variety of topics, shaping, editing , and reworking texts in a range of genres, expressing ideas and experiences imaginatively and using appropriate vocabulary and conventions, such as spelling and sentence structure	• write instructions, explanations, and factual accounts, and express and explain a point of view, in a range of authentic contexts, organising and linking ideas logically and making language choices appropriate to the audience
Level 5	• write regularly and confidently to respond to a range of experiences, ideas, observations, and texts, developing a personal voice	• write on a variety of topics, shaping, editing, and reworking texts in an extended range of genres, selecting appropriate language features and using conventions of writing accurately and confidently	• write coherent, logical instructions, explanations, and factual accounts, and express and argue a point of view, linking main and supporting ideas, and structuring material in appropriate styles in a range of authentic contexts
Level 6	• write regularly, confidently, and fluently to reflect on a range of experiences, ideas, feelings, and texts, developing a personal voice	• write on a variety of topics, shaping, editing, and reworking texts to express experiences and ideas imaginatively in an extended range of genres, choosing appropriate language features and using conventions of writing accurately and with discrimination	• write clear, coherent instructions, explanations, and factual reports and express and justify a point of view persuasively, structuring material confidently, in appropriate styles for different audiences, in a range of authentic contexts
Level 7	• write regularly, confidently, and fluently to reflect on, interpret, and explore a wide range of experiences, ideas, feelings, and texts, developing a personal voice	• write on a variety of topics, shaping, editing, and reworking texts to investigate and explore ideas imaginatively in a wide range of genres, using the conventions of writing securely, and integrating techniques with purpose	• write clear, coherent explanations and reports, and debate a proposition or point of view, structuring well researched material effectively, in appropriate styles for different audiences, in a range of authentic contexts
Level 8	• use expressive writing regularly, fluently, and by choice, to reflect on, interpret, and explore a wide range of experiences, ideas, feelings, and texts, expressing complex thoughts in a personal voice.	• write on a variety of topics, in a wide range of genres, shaping, editing, and reworking texts and demonstrating depth of thought, imaginative awareness, and secure use of language, including accurate and discriminating use of the conventions of writing, and integrating techniques with purpose.	• write explanations and reports on complex issues, and debate in depth a proposition or point of view, structuring well researched material effectively, in appropriate styles for different audiences, in a range of authentic contexts.

Phase 2: Experimental writing

At this phase, children realise that 'speech can be written down and that written messages remain constant'. Five typical indicators of phase 2 are:

the writer – reads back own writing

– uses left to right and top to bottom orientation of print

– demonstrates one-to-one correspondence between written and spoken words

– relies heavily on the most obvious sounds of the word

– writes using simplified language structures.

Phase 2 writing	I LiKe r ꓭ n [I like reading]

Phase 3: Early writing

At this phase, children write personally significant messages, and show some sense of sentence concept. Spelling is mostly phonetic. Typical indicators of phase 3 are:

the writer – is beginning to use narrative structure

Phase 3 writing
My pet is a goat. She is wigte. I feyd my pet ones a day. her name is Sandey. She is very friendle and soft. She is blak and wigte and clean. She livse in a ben.

– experiments with words drawn from language experience activities

– rewrites known stories in sequence

– attempts to use some punctuation

– chooses letters on the basis of sound, without regard for conventional spelling patterns.

Phase 4: Conventional writing

At this phase, children are familiar with most aspects of the writing process, and are able to select forms to suit different purposes. Spelling is approximating the conventional (independent) phase.

The writer – uses a variety of simple, compound and extended sentences

– punctuates simple sentences correctly

– demonstrates knowledge of differences between narrative and informational text when writing

– groups sentences into paragraphs

– uses adverbs and adjectives to enhance meaning

– uses a range of strategies for planning, revising and publishing own written texts.

Phase 4 writing

Dear Mr. and Mrs McKeown

Thank you for helping on all the trips but one. I thought all those trips were fabulus. You were lucky though you went on all the good ones. I learned lots and lots on the trips. I loved being in your group. I liked mapping the view at goat Island and Mt Victoria. It was really tiring walking up Mt Victoria, but when we got to the top it was worth it.

You were wonderful on all the trips and I hope you can come again.

Yours sincerly.   Katie

Phase 5: Proficient writing

At this phase, writers have developed a personal style of writing. They have control over spelling and punctuation. They choose from a wide vocabulary, and their writing is cohesive, coherent and satisfying. Typical indicators are:

the writer – selects text forms to suit purpose and audience, demonstrating control over most essential elements

Phase 5 writing

Magazine Article

An Inexpensive way to live in Luxury.

The Snowview Chateau has a glamerous situation on the edge of a snow covered mountain. Beginners field only a few steps away. Ideal for any starter. For more experienced skiers just a mere 100 yard up the road. After a day of skying come into our warm cozy Chateau. Reliable central heating. Activities in the evenings and a warm 90° pool inside for guests to bathe in free. _ _ _

 – writes a topic sentence and includes relevant information to develop a cohesive paragraph
 – demonstrates accurate use of punctuation
 – chooses appropriate words to create atmosphere and mood
 – edits own writing during and after composing.

Phase 6: Advanced writing

At this phase, writers have effective control over the language and structural features of a large repertoire of text forms. Typical indicators are:

the writer – develops ideas and information clearly, sustaining coherence throughout complex texts
 – uses abstract and technical terms appropriately in context
 – may choose to manipulate or abandon conventional text forms to achieve impact
 – takes responsibility for planning, revising and proof-reading to ensure that writing achieves its purpose
 – reflects on, critically evaluates and critiques own writing and that of others.

Conclusion

The selected indicators listed above in the New Zealand and Western Australian schemes, show some of the ways in which students may develop from one phase or level to the next. However, they vary from day to day, and from one topic to the next, so the authors of the Western Australian scheme advise against the use of such a model to make formal evaluations of children's writing. The criteria are too non-specific to allow for teachers in different schools to be consistent when different topics are set for formal writing, and the conditions under which they are written are not standardised.

The purpose of the schemes are for non-formal diagnostic teaching to help teachers become sensitive to the phases of development which many students pass through, and to help them to nudge the students gently up to the next, with target checklists and conferences. We are concerned that such frameworks are still too vague and ambiguous to be used as a basis for summative assessment where accountability is at stake. Overseas experience indicates that high-stakes assessment is fraught with problems of coaching, biased grading, and cheating, especially where the criteria are vague and not standardised. A pedagogical tool that is useful to guide formative assessment can be counter-productive if it is used in high-stakes assessment for school or teacher accountability.

We fully expect such developmental schemes to be revised and reformulated, as more research is done and teachers devise better ways to observe the significant milestones in children's growth in writing.

The evaluation of writing

'In order to evaluate writing with any degree of satisfaction, first we must ask ourselves, "What is my instructional purpose in this assignment?"'
S. Bratcher, (1994) Evaluating Children's Writing

Many teachers dislike evaluating their pupils' writing. The idea of mutilating a child's page by marking spelling errors and lapses in punctuation with red ink, as traditionalists have done for decades, or putting a discouraging 'C'- grade on a child's best effort, is inconsistent with a teacher's self-image as a praising, constructive agent of good writing processes, alert to identify incipient signs of progress. The harmful effects upon a child who has struggled with an original piece of writing, only to have it returned with every spelling mistake and grammatical error crossed out, together with an unwelcome letter or numerical grade at the bottom, can best be imagined. Perhaps these evaluation techniques have helped create a generation of adults who avoid writing unless it is absolutely necessary.

In order to assess writing we must know what constitutes 'good' writing. Most teachers feel that they are able to identify good writing but are hard-pressed to define the qualities that make writing good, as opposed to adequate. Definitions of good writing hinge on ill-defined terms such as 'liveliness' or 'suitable for its audience'. Again, most teachers feel they can recognise these aspects of writing when they occur (or are aware of their absence in poorer writing) but cannot give concise definitions of the qualities that make them 'lively' or 'appropriate for the audience'.

A major problem we face is that our knowledge of how writing develops in children has outstripped our knowledge of how best to assess that development. Effective measures of writing have not grown in tandem with our deepening understanding of the process.

How can we retain the positive, encouraging approach to children's writing and still fulfil our obligations to parents and administrators for information about performance levels? To do this, we must first and foremost differentiate clearly between the different purposes of assessment. Sometimes assessment is informal, formative and constructive – a private dialogue between teacher and child. At other times, but rarely, it may be necessary to provide a summative grade on a formally assessed piece of writing. For most writing done in the primary school years, the purpose of assessment should be formative and constructive. We should be encouraging children to write regularly, responding helpfully to the ideas they are grappling with, and avoiding the creation of the inhibitions which follow the overuse of the judgemental red pencil. Indeed, many writers on the subject recommend no formal grading of children's writing at all in primary school. The New Zealand Curriculum Statement for English states that assessment of students' progress is essentially diagnostic... its primary purpose is to improve student learning and the quality of a learner's programme. As Frank Smith reminded us 'grading never taught a writer anything' (1988, p. 30). The evidence we quoted in Chapter 5 about negative attitudes to writing among students, after the first four years of school, suggests that there is much to be gained from avoiding those disheartening summative assessments in the form of grades or marks for as long as possible. We do not want the positive feelings built up with enlightened process writing undermined by an evaluation policy which leaves the children's efforts 'awash in a sea of red ink'.

Most writing sessions, then, are aimed at improving children's writing with constructive comments, and for such aims, the assessments made should be formative and diagnostic, rather than summative and judgemental. In other words, the main purpose of assessment in writing should be forward-looking, rather than backward-looking. Therefore the focus of this chapter is on formative assessment strategies.

Formative assessment

The main aim of formative assessment is to help a student to improve, to progress from his/her present level of development to higher levels. Such assessment is most helpful when it is focused on particular points, or is given constructively, and addresses the writing, rather than the student. Our comments should be pitched at the child's own level, if we are to communicate the messages we want taken on board.

To help a student progress, it is important for teachers to be aware of the major milestones of children's writing development so that evaluation can be realistic and tailored to the pupil's current needs. (See Chapter 14.) If Charles is functioning at the precommunicative stage of spelling, and dislikes writing, we do not discourage him further by emphasising his spelling difficulties when we have finally succeeded in getting him to write a paragraph about his fishing expedition. If Vicky has only just worked out where to put full-stops, we do not then challenge her to cope with the apostrophe in plural nouns. But we would try to help her with question marks, if she shows such a need.

Formative assessments in the classroom can be carried out in a variety of ways. These are listed below with examples of each kind.

1   Conferencing

A one-to-one conference between teacher and child during the writing period offers much potential for diagnosing weaknesses and providing constructive ideas for improvement. Here the feedback is normally oral, with the pupil taking an important role, to ensure that he/she maintains ownership of the writing. The Ministry of Education handbook, *Dancing with the Pen*, points out that conferences have an important role to play in helping writers 'recognise what they already know as something worth writing about' (1992, p. 45).

Conferencing is also important for clarifying the writing. Often, emergent writers do not recognise that writing must set out the assumptions that are implicit in speech. *Dancing with the Pen* expresses it this way:

> *'Often the writers have not expressed all that is necessary to communicate what they wish to say about a topic. It is important for them to realise that the reader only has the words on the page to work with. Encouraging learners to talk with each other often makes the gaps or confusions clear.'*
> (1992, p. 45)

The teacher may guide the development of the conference with predictable questions such as:

'Tell me what you wrote about.'
'Which part are you most pleased with?'
'Which part is causing you trouble?'

Conferencing is a clearly developed concept from Graves' work and is discussed in more detail in Chapter 6.

2   *Checklists*

Checklists, as the name implies, are intended to list important indicators that teachers and students can use to check off when the behaviour is mastered, partially or fully. They are useful to tell at a glance, during conferences, at what stage a student's writing is, and where effort is required. They provide intermediate goals, and knowledge of progress for the learner, without causing excessive rivalry with others. They are also valuable for assisting children to take more responsibility for their own learning. The criteria to consider in assessing and improving are made very clear, and once students start assessing their own writing, in relation to such agreed-upon criteria, they are well on the way to becoming mature writers. One should be cautious, of course, about the assumption that learning a set of unrelated skills means good quality overall. This is not always the case.

Checklists come in many forms. They may provide a straight list of behaviours, with a space for checking off when they are mastered. Here the assumption is that each behaviour is of equal importance, and that mastery is an all-or-nothing matter. Both assumptions are of dubious validity. However, such checklists do have the advantage of speed and simplicity for busy teachers.

More elaborate, but time-consuming checklists require the teachers to rate the student's behaviour on a two-point scale, as partially or fully mastered, or even on a four-point scale, ranging from *Excellent* to *Incomplete*. Sometimes the behaviours are grouped into related categories, arranged in order of priority, and even given different weights. They may be tailor-made for students or for particular kinds of writing, or general for all students and writing exercises. Examples of this kind of checklist are given in Table 9.

Table 9 – *Phase 3: Early writing*

Name: .... Date: ....

Look what I can do	not yet	sometimes	always
• Choose interesting things to write about.			
• Explain why I am writing.			
• Write recounts, procedures, stories, letters, lists, labels, signs and other interesting things that I need to write.			
• Find some parts of my writing that need to be improved.			
• Mark some words in my writing that I am not sure of.			
• Talk about my plans for writing.			
• Re-read my writing to make sure it makes sense.			
• Use our class checklist to help me edit my work.			
• Share my ideas for writing.			
• Listen to other people's writing and make suggestions to improve it.			
• Sound-out words.			
• Use word banks and class charts to help me with my spelling when I write.			
I like	**not yet**	**sometimes**	**always**
• writing for fun			
• being able to finish my writing			
• to see others enjoy my stories			
• showing others what I write			
• talking about what I am going to write.			

3 Portfolios

Teachers and students like to see progress in writing performance. One increasingly popular method is to collect samples of student writing at different times, and store them in portfolios, one for each child. These portfolios may be folders with pockets or accordion files which are expandable. Students can store examples of their writing in different genres (narrative, expository, letters, poems, etc.) in one portfolio or have different portfolios for each area where writing is commonly done, perhaps colour-coded for each content area. Some portfolio systems include all written work done; others include only those pieces of writing judged to be good.

An important advantage of the portfolio is that it can reveal at a glance the progress made by students over time, in style, handwriting, vocabulary, spelling, layout or any other feature of interest. Students can participate in selecting samples of writing for inclusion, and inspecting the samples over a period of time with teachers or parents, and become personally involved in studying progress and setting new goals. Such virtues will do much to encourage children to take responsibility for their own improvement.

Another benefit is that the 'before and after' perspective, encouraged by portfolios, reduces the need for formal grades and within-class competition. The natural question 'How am I doing?' can be answered by pointing to areas where progress is clear and others where it is not.

There are obvious advantages in being selective about including everything written by students. They may feel inhibited about experimenting, if they believe their work could be ridiculed by others. Also, portfolios that include everything become too bulky and time-consuming to organise. Students should have some freedom to discard what they are not proud of. However, class guidelines will be necessary, or some students will want to reject too much of their writing.

4   Peer evaluation

Evaluation of students' writing can become time-consuming if teachers attempt to read and comment on everything that is written in the class. One method of reducing unrealistic marking loads is to involve a student's own classmates from time to time in formative evaluation exercises. This may be done by having students read aloud to the class or small groups from their writing. Another approach is to work in pairs where students exchange papers and read to comment on particular criteria which are agreed to beforehand. It is usually easier to organise paired assessment before working in groups.

There are some dangers in peer group evaluation, as some students may be unduly harsh in their criticisms, and cause discouragement, even resentment. However, the risks can be minimised by modelling, teacher-led discussion, and guidelines on appropriate comments to make and prior agreement on the criteria to use. It is useful for teachers to demonstrate, using real examples of anonymous writing collected from other classes, and discussed with the class. Most children can readily learn to comment on aspects such as the parts that they like best, whether introductions and conclusions are clear, or particular conventions observed. Students may be less able to evaluate the overall piece of writing. The experience of collectively working out criteria to use for particular writing exercises, and then applying them in a group, before attempting to discuss others' writing should itself be a growing point for many students. Teachers need to supervise this approach carefully, and to ensure that a constructive learning atmosphere predominates over a judgemental one. There is potential for growth for all when children read one another's work in a positive environment, looking for suggestions that are intended to help. And those whose work is assessed gain more experience at realising what various audiences expect. It is an important step towards understanding the needs of the reader.

5   Self-evaluation

All students evaluate their work informally as they write. But if we take seriously the aim of making them responsible for their own progress, we should often ask them to evaluate their own work as a whole, and record their comments for discussion with teacher or peers, especially when the emphasis is on formative assessment, and the stakes are not high. However, some teachers do have students assess their own work and use the self-assessments as a basis for discussion before making their own formal evaluation.

Ideally, the student should be involved in deciding on the criteria to use, deciding which pieces of writing to assess, and at what stage of the process (first draft, publication format) to make the assessment.

Once again, the whole process should be modelled and discussed with the class beforehand. For many children, it is a revelation to discover that expert writers actually question their own writing, that crossings-out and reordering are part of the normal process and that there is value in hearing the responses of others to our writing because they make us think again and try a different tack.

Children can be encouraged to identify parts that they like in their own writing, parts that need further attention, phrases that may be unclear, or words that are overused (see p. 76). They can check such things as paragraphing and variety of sentence openings, or structures, and whether there is a capital letter and full stop for each sentence.

Not all students adapt to this form of evaluation, and some parents may need to be educated about its merits. But used judiciously, it has much to offer in sensitising students to the strengths and weaknesses of their own writing, and making them feel responsible for their own progress.

Summative evaluation

The reality in most schools is that parents or principals usually expect some form of grades, levels or marks to indicate how students are progressing in their writing. A formal survey may be conducted at the end of term, and teachers will be expected to standardise conditions and arrange for a formal piece of writing to be undertaken by all. This formal type of assessment, to produce grades for external reporting purposes, at the end of a unit or a school term, is referred to as 'summative.' Some educators describe it as 'high stakes' assessment as the implications for students who do not do well are often far-reaching. And if the school is required to report trends and averages, such assessment may have implications for the public perception of the teachers and even for judgements about quality and school reputation.

If summative assessment is required, it is still important to allow some choice in what students write about. Few students can show what they are capable of if they are unmoved by the topic. But there are some aspects which should be the same for all – advance notice of the task, amount of help from home or peers, first draft or second, time allowed to complete and the criteria used in assessing should be understood by all. Such matters should be standardised if the results are to be valid.

How to get maximum reliability

One of the major problems in summative assessment in writing is that it is notoriously unreliable. When students write once only, on a single topic, and their work is marked once by a teacher, the reliability rarely reaches 0.6. This means that a second writing effort, on a different topic, and graded by a different teacher, would produce somewhat different results. About one third of students who were above (say) the average for the first occasion would fall below it on the second. This finding is well documented in research, and some studies show that an adequate level of reliability requires about six assessments – three essays marked by two people, or two essays marked by three people (Elley et al., 1979). This recommendation may not be a practicable solution in a busy classroom, but it is a useful reminder that for high-stakes summative assessments, when the future of individual students may be affected, that there should be more than one writing task, and that there should be more than one marker.

Why is reliability such a problem?

First, students' general writing competence is variable, from day to day and from topic to topic – much more so than in homogeneous skills like spelling or handwriting or computational skills. Students may write a brilliant, entertaining story about 'Breakfast at my place' today and a tired rehash of a class discussion on 'Why we should have school uniforms' the next day. Such variability could be reduced by grading students on only one genre of writing at a time – narrative writing this term, expository next term, or by separating the genres in some other way.

Secondly, there are many criteria to apply in assessing fairly. Some teachers emphasise surface features – spelling, handwriting, punctuation – while others focus more on whether the content is relevant, logically presented or interesting. Others again are heavily influenced by the style and vocabulary choice, others by how much the writing shows improvement from the last formal assessment made. Such criteria should be discussed in staff rooms in order to develop a school policy related to age and local needs, and this policy should be explained to students in terms they can understand, for the particular tasks set. For younger children, criteria such as legibility, length and message clarity may take precedence. For older students, sentence structure, quality of ideas, usage and appropriate use of conventions would normally play a greater part. The criteria may change also according to topic and genre, to the level of the students' development (see Chapter 14) and according to whether the writing is in the first draft or not.

A third factor which reduces reliability in grading is the subjectivity inherent in judging quality. It is easy to count spelling errors or lapses in punctuation, but factors such as style, interest, creativity and consideration of audience, for instance, are intangible and uncountable. What one teacher regards as a creative idea may be judged nonsensical by another. Hence the need for using more than one assessor, and bringing in a third person where there are obvious discrepancies in judgements. If this suggestion is impractical, it may still be possible to appeal to a second person's judgement where there is a marked difference between the grades assigned to certain students and the quality of their writing throughout the term.

All these differences in values are serious sources of unreliability. Indeed, the differences between countries in the weight they give to various assessment criteria have so far made it impossible for valid international comparisons of students' writing ability, such as have occurred in reading, mathematics and science.

Which grading system is better – holistic or analytic?

Some teachers prefer a holistic or impressionistic approach when marking essays. They read through each student's contribution, place them in three or more piles according to their overall impression, and make a tentative grading. They then repeat the process, comparing the essays in each pile and refining their judgement with pluses or minuses, or moving them up or down a pile. No attempt is made, in holistic grading, to identify the specific criteria, and to assign marks to each.

Other teachers are more meticulous. They spell out the criteria they wish to use, and analyse each essay by allocating a mark to each one. They may weight them differently according to their importance, then total them. Typical criteria for analytic marking are:

1 **Content:** Sufficient, appropriate, relevant, interesting.

2 **Organisation:** Sequencing, clear beginning and ending, paragraphing.

3 **Style:** word choice, originality, suitability for audience, variation in structures.

4 **Mechanics:** Spelling, punctuation, sentence structure, grammar.

Strangely enough, comparative research has not shown that analytic grading is superior to holistic. Thus, if many essays are to be assessed in a formal examination, and students are not expecting to receive feedback, the holistic approach is more efficient. However, if the assessment is intended to provide feedback, or some kind of diagnostic information is intended, an analytical approach is normally preferred. It has potential to provide more useful information to teachers and students.

How can marking schemes help?

If analytic marking is adopted, a marking scheme is to be recommended. Such a scheme should list the criteria, in a convenient way for assigning marks, and allot appropriate weights for each. For instance, Paul Diederich's widely used scheme (see Table 10) has the obvious merit of convenience of use (Diederich, 1974, p. 54).

Table 10 – Marking scheme for summative assessment

General Merit	Low		Middle		High
Ideas	2	4	6	8	10
Organisation	2	4	6	8	10
Wording	2	4	6	8	10
Flavour	2	4	6	8	10
Mechanics					
Usage	2	4	6	8	10
Punctuation	2	4	6	8	10
Spelling	2	4	6	8	10
Handwriting	2	4	6	8	10

Other schemes provide descriptive labels to assist the marker to focus consistently on the various criteria. An example for general usage is given below (Table 11). Particular writing tasks may warrant some adaptation.

Table 11 – Marking scheme based on descriptors

Grade	Clarity of message	Mechanics
5	Message effectively conveyed with no gaps/redundancies	Faultless grammar, spelling and punctuation
4	Message effectively conveyed with occasional gaps/redundancies	Good use of grammar, occasional lapses in spelling or punctuation
3	Message broadly conveyed but lacking in structure or flow	Enough errors in grammar or spelling or punctuation to suggest misconceptions
2	Message unclear. Many gaps and deficiencies	Some glaring faults in grammar, spelling or punctuation
1	No coherent message decipherable	Content incoherent due to poor grammar, spelling or punctuation

It is wise to regard marking guides as tentative until a sample of essays has been read.

Further suggestions for improving the summative assessment of writing

The following recommendations have common sense or research findings to support them.

1   Give students ample warning of the forthcoming assessment, and some guidance on how to prepare themselves.

2   Ensure that the writing tasks set are appropriate and clearly understood. There are many anecdotes which suggest that wording which is clear to the teacher is often interpreted differently by students.

3   Allow students some choice of topic, to ensure that they can show themselves to good advantage.

4   Inform students beforehand of the criteria of evaluation, and their respective weighting, if any.

5   Ask a teaching colleague to critique one's proposed writing task for clarity and the appropriateness of the criteria used in assessing.

6   Before grading, read a small sample of essays to note typical approaches taken and standards expected.

7   Mark all the essays on one topic together, before starting another. Otherwise one's standards of grading are more likely to change.

8   Use more than one marker where possible, and conceal the mark given by the first marker. Alternatively, mark each essay twice, with a time lapse between sessions, and change the sequence in which they are marked. When two assessments of the same piece of writing disagree, obtain a third judgement.

9   Stick closely to the criteria agreed beforehand.

10   For important examinations, mark anonymously where possible, i.e., without knowledge of the student's identity.

11   Form some defensible policy on how to handle incomplete essays, misinterpreted questions, barely legible writing or word processing. Such policies should be related to the overall purpose of the assessment, and its role in students' future schooling.

Early writing assessment

Clay (1975) has compiled a useful technique for the formal rating of progress in early writing, during the first six months at school. She suggests that three samples of written work should be collected over three days or closely together. The analysis is based on three broad criteria – language level, message quality and directional principles (see Table 12).

Clay also proposes keeping a record of writing vocabulary by asking children to write down all the words they know, starting with their own name. This technique has the virtue of being simple to administer and score – a simple tally of words correctly written will suffice, although if the sheets are kept, a comprehensive developmental record of the child's progress exists.

Table 12 – *Rating scheme for early writing (from Clay, 1975, pp. 66–67).*

Language level
1 Alphabetic (letters only)
2 Word (any recognisable word)
3 Word group (any two-word phrase)
4 Sentence (any simple sentence)
5 Punctuated story (of two or more sentences)
6 Paragraphed story (two themes)

Message quality: Record the number below for the best description of the child's sample.
1 He has a concept of signs (uses letters, invents letters, uses punctuation).
2 He has a concept that the message is conveyed (i.e. he tells you about a message but what he has written is not that message).
3 A message is copied, and he knows more or less what that message says.
4 Repetitive, independent use of sentence patterns like 'here is a...'
5 Attempts to record own ideas, mostly independently.
6 Successful composition.

Directional principles: Record the number of the highest rating for which there is no error in the sample of the child's writing.
1 No evidence of directional knowledge
2 Part of the directional pattern is known

	Either	start top left
	Or	Move left to right
	Or	Return down left

3 Reversal of the directional pattern (right to left and/or return down right). A sample with one lapse should be rated at this level.
4 Correct directional pattern.
5 Correct directional pattern and spaces between words.
6 Extensive text without any difficulties of arrangement and spacing of text.

 Responsive evaluation

Another coherent method of summative assessment has been developed by Cambourne and Turbill (1990) in collaboration with a number of teachers who were co-researchers. They refer to their system as 'Responsive evaluation' which is based on the principles underlying whole language teaching. The teacher gathers appropriate information by responding to the students who are being evaluated. This means that the children are talked to, they are observed working, and outcomes of their work are collected. The teacher's philosophy of how writing is taught underpins the decision about what information to collect. Cambourne and Turbill's scheme calls for information to be collected in five broad categories, namely

1 the strategies children use for reading and writing

2 the level of explicit understanding learners have of the processes they are using

3 the learner's attitudes towards reading and writing

4   the learner's interests and backgrounds

5   the degree of control that learners display over language in all its forms (p. 342).

The first four categories rely on simple observation. Category 5 is more complex and requires the teacher to develop what Cambourne and Turbill refer to as 'markers' – overt forms of language behaviours that mark or give evidence of the presence of some kind of linguistic skill or attribute (p. 343). Included in the markers are items such as a sense of audience, appropriate use of language conventions, range of genre, and so on. The content of these categories changes as the children progress through the year, and through the school grades.

Once data has been collected it has to be synthesised. The form the synthesis takes will depend on the audience for the information. Thus, a report to parents will be perhaps more discursive than a report to a school principal or a review by an outside agency. The researchers suggest that the time commitment for teachers to use responsive evaluation techniques is no greater, and may actually be less, than the time involved in traditional assessment methods.

Cambourne and Turbill concede that the normal strictures about reliability and validity do not fit neatly into a responsive evaluation model. However, they argue that by adhering to specified criteria for credibility, transferability, dependability, and conformability, data obtained by a process of responsive evaluation is as reliable and valid as data obtained by more traditional methods. Cambourne and Turbill express this view forcefully (p. 346):

'data from a more naturalistic, responsive approach to assessment are not only more useful, rich and valuable than sterile numbers but … they are equally rigorous, trustworthy and scientific.'

 ## Summary

Teachers have an obligation to assess their students' writing. For most legitimate purposes, assessment should be informal and constructive. It should be carried out in such a way as to help students move forward, and to retain a positive view of writing. Teachers who know their students, and are aware of the key developmental milestones in their students' writing, should find ample opportunities to achieve their objectives in conferences with the aid of checklists, portfolios, and help from other members of the class. A useful aim to keep in mind is making each student responsible for his/her own improvement.

When summative evaluation is necessary, for external reporting, there are numerous guidelines to observe to gain maximum reliability and validity – which can often be problematic in the case of writing. Marking criteria should be clear to students and consistently applied by teachers. Cambourne and Turbill (1990) have developed a promising scheme of responsive evaluation, designed to broaden the basis of writing assessment, and to include processes and attitudes, as well as products.

The role of the teacher

'Good teaching is forever being on the cutting edge of the child's competence.'
J. Bruner, (1986) Actual Minds, Possible Words

We have made a long journey in this book – from the delights of the anecdotes reported by the advocates of a process approach to writing, to the clinical precision of the behavioural psychologists; from the joys of the spontaneous utterances of preschoolers to the tedium of learning one's spelling lists. The reader who has persevered with us to this stage now can rightfully demand of us – where do we stand? How should adults teach children to write? What is our final statement on how best to help children towards a love of writing? This chapter pulls together the central threads of the messages contained in each chapter, and attempts to provide some coherence for teachers of writing.

Knowing how the child develops

Teachers are responsible for educating children – so they should have sound assumptions about how children develop. We have shown how the very young child is a social being, immersed in a sea of language from birth, and surrounded by people who respond to the first gurgles, and then to the first words. These people continue to respond, also, to the tangled, lengthy utterances of the toddler, expanding them with more language of their own. In this ocean of words there is one important constant – the people in the immediate environment, people that respond to the **content** of the child's utterances, to **what** is being said, first, and only then to **how** it is said. In our view meaning should – and usually does – take precedence over form.

Later, within the family environment, the young child makes the first tentative steps towards beginning to write. Research shows that, given a model and an opportunity, young children attempt to write stories, construct lists, write letters to their relatives, and engage in a host of other 'writing' activities. That many adults dismiss these efforts as mere 'play' is a result of their inability to recognise the power of imitative play to lead the child readily towards a form of writing that is accepted by the world of adults. Authentic purposes provide the best springboard even if they are fanciful.

Then, at age five (or six or seven, depending on the country) there is a major change in the life of the young child. Compulsory school attendance begins. Attending school enlarges the circle of significant adults in the child's life to include a teacher who is more distant from the child's family than the adults encountered regularly in preschool life. The teacher is expected to teach the young child to write, and the manner in which this task is approached will be crucial in determining whether the child grows into a confident, willing and successful writer or one for whom writing is difficult and unrewarding.

There is no simple solution to this task. No programme, or prepackaged box of tricks, exists which will enable all children to become successful writers. We learn from people. How people demonstrate language and respond to children's efforts does make a huge difference.

Reading the research

Teachers are pragmatic – they use what works. We believe that all the research presented in this book has something to offer teachers in their daily classroom work. Moreover, we submit, the ideas presented here are not incompatible in practice. At first reading, perhaps, an applied behaviourist approach appears to have little in common with a process approach. But if we examine a key idea of Graves' – that of the writing conference – we find it can be aptly understood in terms of a behaviourist paradigm. A conference should be supportive of what the writer is trying to say. To use the language of the behaviourist, it should be positively reinforcing. In practice, it has the same outcome.

Pragmatic teaching should also be based on an understanding of the results of research, because some practices, while apparently based on common sense ideas, do not actually assist children to write. Common sense would suggest that instruction and practice exercises in formal grammar will improve the quality of children's writing. Research shows that typically it will not. Common sense would suggest that correcting all the mistakes in children's stories will improve the quality of their writing. Research shows that it will not. Common sense would suggest that spelling is best learned from a daily study of word lists. Research shows that it is not. Generations of children have been turned off writing by such counter-productive traditional methods. We can surely do better. To claim that our classroom practices are pragmatic means that we know what works and under what conditions it is successful. And in order to know what works, researchers have had to analyse carefully the children's writing and the teacher's actions and establish how one affects the other.

In this book, we have outlined and used a number of research paradigms, each of which emphasises differing aspects of writing. Behaviourism focuses on the individual, and his/her reactions to changes in the environment. The stress here is upon objectivity and careful quantifying of what is happening. By contrast, whole language advocates typically use significant anecdotes to examine classroom practices, and to reveal insights into children's thinking. Both paradigms have their place in the writing research. So does the work of the cognitive psychologists. We would not wish to rule out any source of evidence in the quest for better writers. It is important that the teacher understands and can draw evidence from each paradigm in order to improve his/her classroom practice.

Understanding the role of curriculum

Our approach to writing has as its central core a relevant curriculum taught with sound pedagogical methods. By curriculum we mean all the formal aspects of a school programme – art, music, science, health, physical education, mathematics, social studies, reading. These are the disciplines which serve as the organising factor in the daily life of the classroom. Curriculum content, and the ways in which it is studied, should determine much of the content of a writing programme. It provides the raw material of knowledge. Writing is always about something – feelings, facts and opinions or combinations of each. It has purpose – to entertain, to educate, to persuade, to question. The subject of the writing and its purpose are drawn mostly from the wider school curriculum.

In the past, much formal writing at school has lacked a clear purpose – to the children at least. The teacher may have had a purpose but it may not have been clear to the children. Hood's (1994) survey in New Zealand primary schools found that most children did not understand their teachers' goals in writing. The teacher may want her class to write more complex sentences, but to the children it may appear that all they are being expected to do is to write the same thing using more words.

We see writing that emerges from a curriculum unit such as health or social studies, as more likely to have a purpose that is obvious to the children. For example, in a science area, children's questions can be posed in writing – 'Where does the electricity go when you turn off the switch?'. The question may be asked in a letter to an electrical engineer, as a question to classmates and teacher, or in a puzzle embedded in a story. The reply may be found in answers to the letter, or as a result of a careful search through encyclopedias or by interviewing a knowledgeable person. The reply can be recorded on a wall story for everyone to read, or kept in a folder of personal writing as private information.

Essential to this process, then, is a skilled teacher who can endow children with a sense of curiosity to go on a journey to find out about themselves, their homes, their school, their community, their country and their world and to record their travels in some way. The curriculum is the organising factor which allows such sweeping aims to be broken into manageable chunks.

We do not downplay the importance of children's writing of personal narrative. They must have the opportunity to write about themselves, especially in the junior school. But all too often the cry, 'I've got nothing to write about' is a result of the misinterpretation of Graves' concept of daily practice and ownership of the topic. We actually favour some directed writing amidst the personal choice routines. We consider that writing as a result of specified curriculum topics is as legitimate as personal writing.

We know that preschoolers like to write, using a range of media and genres. We also know that during their first years of school there is a reduction in children's enthusiasm, both in the amount that they write, and in the genres used. While schools cannot duplicate the home environment, neither should they ignore it. Research into family literacy suggests that a wide array of literacy practices (both reading and writing) are common among all groups in society. Yet many children find a disjunction between family and school writing practices. Skills learned at home are not often recognised or valued by the school. To many children, writing at school has become a tedious task, removed from a meaningful context and lacking a discernible purpose. Schools have an obligation to see what children can do, and to build on that.

Both Vygotsky and McNaughton drew our attention to the central role that society plays in children's learning. We learn first from our interactions with people around us; then, when we have internalised these processes, from our internal thoughts. Therefore, to be effective, school curricula should be derived from society around us. The concerns of our communities should be the concerns of our curricula, and not those derived from an abstract curriculum as specified by a text book, written and published all too often by a committee, with scant regard to the needs of the society in which it is to be used.

Effective teaching of writing thus eschews the use of pre-packaged exercises which children work through in a fixed sequence. These exercises lack meaningful context or personal purpose for the child. An effective writing programme, based on a school curriculum in New York, will therefore be different from a curriculum-based programme in an Auckland or Honiara classroom. The underlying pedagogy will be similar, but the content of the writing will inevitably be different.

There is no shortage of things to learn about in life. We are learning all the time and usually we are unaware that we are learning. Only in formal schooling does learning come to be associated with hard work, boredom and the possibility of failure. The school curriculum that values the ability to parse sentences correctly above the ability to write a cheer-up letter to a sick classmate, or the ability to commit to memory long lists of irrelevant spelling words rather than to design a poster advertising the school fair, such a curriculum is in danger of turning the spontaneous activity of learning into a dreary task. We hold no personal antagonism towards grammar or spelling. They are worthy objects of study, provided they are studied to answer children's questions. We object to them only as elements of an abstract and irrelevant curriculum. It is in such an atmosphere that many children find writing difficult. No clear, discernible purpose exists for it. The chance of failure is high.

A pedagogy of writing

All this does not mean that the teacher's sole function is to provide a lively curriculum. It is not enough to provide the motivation for children to write and then to leave them alone to get on with it. We do not advocate a *laissez-faire* attitude to writing instruction.

It is the teacher's clear responsibility to assist children with their writing – to guide them from being insecure novices to becoming fluent, confident authors. Here the teacher can draw upon a rich body of research for help. From Graves we have learned of the need for the writer to 'own' the topic, for regular daily writing, feedback and publishing for a real audience. From Cambourne we learned the importance of immersing children in print, of encouraging them into writing with demonstrations, joint writing, and lots of talk from a sympathetic audience. From the cognitive psychologists we gained some insights into the way writers tackle their task, what barriers children face, and some helpful ideas for overcoming them. The applied behaviourists produced strong evidence for supporting children's efforts with appropriate comments about the content of their writing.

These, and the many other insights reported in each chapter, have often been applied by skilled teachers in the past. Indeed, the observations of such teachers, built on a genuine desire to help, frequently produced enlightened practices that researchers are now confirming. Good practice often precedes research in education. However, with hard data to support them – and more is certainly needed – these practices can rise above the status of changing fads and fashions and individual eccentricities to become authoritative recommendations for all teachers to use, to adapt and to improve on. They can be confidently drawn on in teachers' discussions with colleagues, parents and Boards of Trustees, and serve as pointers to new and better practices.

To help clarify and integrate the various teacher's roles in producing better writers, we have set out a flow chart (Figure 22) to illustrate visually our recommended pedagogy of writing. The figure should be read from left to right. It firstly describes the teacher's own understandings, which allow for the establishment of a particular climate in the classroom. Within this climate, the teacher acts as a facilitator of writing, which in turn leads to supportive responses to the child's efforts, and then to a celebration of the product, and finally to a review of the whole process.

Figure 23 illustrates our model of this process.

Explaining the model

The teaching of writing is a complex undertaking in which the role of the teacher is pivotal. While the end product is the student's work, the teacher has played a number of key roles in its creation. To do this competently, teachers first need a background of knowledge and understanding as is shown in box 1 of the figure. This constitutes the professional memory of teachers, acquired in their training and in their teaching experience.

The first element is **an understanding of the writing process**, how drafting and revising are carried out, and how their own responses affect children's efforts. Much of this book is devoted to developing such an understanding, in particular the chapters on Graves and Cambourne. The second element in box 1 is **teachers' confidence in their own competence with the English language** – its syntax, vocabulary and spelling. Teachers

Figure 3 *The teacher's role in writing*

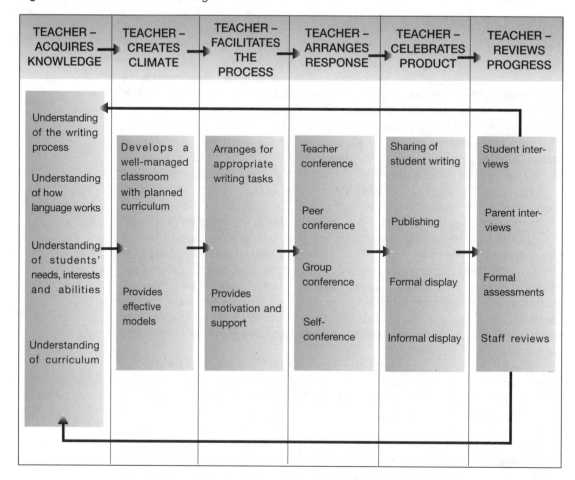

TEACHER – ACQUIRES KNOWLEDGE	TEACHER – CREATES CLIMATE	TEACHER – FACILITATES THE PROCESS	TEACHER – ARRANGES RESPONSE	TEACHER – CELEBRATES PRODUCT	TEACHER – REVIEWS PROGRESS
Understanding of the writing process	Develops a well-managed classroom with planned curriculum	Arranges for appropriate writing tasks	Teacher conference	Sharing of student writing	Student inter-views
Understanding of how language works			Peer conference	Publishing	Parent inter-views
Understanding of students' needs, interests and abilities	Provides effective models	Provides motivation and support	Group conference	Formal display	Formal assessments
Understanding of curriculum			Self-conference	Informal display	Staff reviews

should be good models and be able to give helpful feedback in respect of the children's writing on word choice, structure, tenses and be sure about the corrections they make for publication. It helps too, to keep up with children's fashions in language, to encourage the informal, colourful phrase. Good writing teachers read often, and they write themselves. They enrich their teaching with a wide range of vocabulary and demonstrate an enthusiasm for words and ideas.

The third element is **teachers' knowledge of their own students' needs and abilities** – which of them needs help in formulating a topic, who is fluent and confident, what topics are popular, when to persuade and when to leave alone, how much help to provide, how to approach a conference with each one, which students not to pair up for comments on drafts, and the like. The ability to cope with these daily classroom challenges is enhanced by an understanding of the writing process, but must be supplemented with a detailed and sympathetic understanding of the students in the class.

The fourth element is the teacher's **understanding of the school**

curriculum. This provides the content of much of the classroom writing – it is the raw material of the writing programme and will be derived from the needs and interests of the children and their community. It involves a sure grasp of the aims and developmental levels of children in each area – science, maths, social studies, art, music, health, and physical education, as well as imaginative ideas on how to expand and challenge children's knowledge in these areas.

All of the teacher's knowledge feeds into the second box which describes the classroom climate created through applying this teacher knowledge. The first element describes some important attributes the classroom should display. A **well-managed classroom** is one with established, consistent routines for both behaviour and for cognitive activities with a supportive teacher. The environment is predictable for the class. In such an atmosphere the children will feel secure and able to get on with their work without being distracted by outbursts of bad behaviour from fellow-classmates or because they are unable to find appropriate assistance, when it is needed. Teachers need to be able to organise the classroom to best effect, to motivate, supervise, and assess appropriately, and to ensure that students are suitably challenged and are on task. They need to be able to communicate their intentions, their enthusiasms and their constraints, and maintain sufficient control to allow maximum growth for all.

The second component in creating an effective climate is the **teacher providing suitable models**. Children need to see their teacher writing and sharing his/her writing with them. The influence that a powerful role model such as a teacher can have in a classroom should never be underestimated. Teachers should therefore do their best to provide good models. This means speaking and writing well, and identifying good writing wherever it may be found. It means inviting visitors to the classroom who can serve as role models. It means reading good quality literature to the class and discussing its merits. It means writing *for* the children, as well as writing *with* the children and sometimes writing *to* them. It means collective recording of class discussions, or individual talks, so that students can see how writing is done. It means talking about, evaluating and enthusing about good writing, about apt turns of phrase, vivid adjectives, humorous dialogue and the like.

The third box of the diagram has the teacher acting as a facilitator for the children's writing. This element deserves much careful thought and forward planning. For younger children we support a Graves approach where children are *choosing their own topic* much of the time, but often with gentle guidance from the teacher. This leaves the child in control, and helps maintain motivation (see Chapters 6 and 7 for elaboration).

Frequently, however, writing will arise out of a theme from social studies or science (see Chapter 10 for more on this topic). Such common writing experiences provide ideal opportunities for pre-writing discussion, listing of useful words and ideas, advice on planning, study of models, things to avoid, tricky spelling, and other techniques which will stimulate and bring students' relevant ideas to the surface. Children will thus develop, with the assistance of peers as well as the teacher, appropriate strategies to assist them with their writing, in a variety of genres.

The next phase in the flow chart, **arranging for a response**, is where the teachers' role is most critical. Ideally, teachers should sit with each student at some time during the writing of the first draft, to encourage, to expand, to question, to suggest solutions and to set goals. This conference is at the heart of process writing – to assist during the process (see Chapters 6 and 14). Without help at this stage, improvement is largely a matter of trial and error. This is where the Vygotskian concept of a zone of proximal development is so important. This is where teaching can be tailored to need. This is where teachers can demonstrate, explain, arrange for practice and then gradually transfer responsibility to the learner – at the point of need. In practice, teachers often delegate this task to peers – to groups or individuals or partners – for initial comment, as classes are usually too large and time is too short for daily conferences, but if the climate is right, there is still much to be gained in helping the writer gauge reaction from an audience of peers. Conferences vary in formality and frequency, but good teachers must plan to ensure regular sharing if writing is to improve and so that children can learn to see their writing from the viewpoint of an audience (see Chapters 6, 7 and 8).

Next, there is the act of **celebrating the revised product** in some way. Teachers need to ensure that a fair proportion of each child's work is shared and displayed in the classroom, or sent to an audience, or read aloud to peers or submitted for a newspaper or at least stored in a folder for later reference. Typically, this will entail advising and checking on final copy, assisting with publication, word-processing and lay-out, and arranging for distribution. This celebration stage is a key component in maintaining student motivation, and giving a higher profile to writing in the curriculum.

Finally, the teacher needs to take stock and **review the progress** made by the class. This entails discussing progress and further challenges with individual students; it entails communicating with parents to discuss their children's writing, and where they may be able to assist further growth; occasionally it may require formal assessments under standardised conditions, in order to report individual and class achievement levels, and identify particular strengths and weaknesses. The outcomes of such formal assessments may become part of internal school reviews by teachers of the school writing programme, or perhaps form part of a comprehensive report to the school governing body. It may sometimes be required to provide written reports on individual students. Ideally, the results of such reviews and reporting processes would be fed back into the teacher's knowledge and teaching practices so that the next cycle of the model would be enhanced, and the writing programme improved.

Thus, the teacher's role in helping her/his students write confidently and willingly is a proactive one. It entails much more than the traditional role of setting the topic, suggesting ideas, and marking the results. It is much more creative than the stereotyped instruction in formal grammar and the weekly testing of spelling lists that are a legacy of the past. A vital writing programme requires a talented, well-educated and committed teacher, who enjoys writing and is enthusiastic at every stage of the model.

Bibliography

Ackerman, J. (1993) The Promise of Writing to Learn. *Written Communication.* Vol 10, No 3.

Applebee, A. (1981) Looking at Writing. *Education Leadership.* March pp. 458–462.

Applebee, A. et al. (1986) *The Writing Report Card: Writing Achievement in American Schools.* Educational Testing Service, Princeton.

Arndt, T. (1980) Effects of timing and feedback on output and legibility in story writing. Unpublished research paper in Education. University of Auckland.

Arvidson, G.L. (1960) *Learning to Spell. Studies in Education No. 17.* New Zealand Council for Educational Research, Wellington.

Arvidson, G.L. (1977) *Learning to Spell: A Manual for use with the Alphabetic Spelling List.* New Zealand Council for Education Research, Wellington, New Zealand.

Ashton-Warner, S. (1963) *Teacher.* Bantem Books, New York.

Bangert-Drowns, R. (1993) The Word Processor as an Instructional Tool: A Meta-Analysis of Word Processing in Writing Instruction. *Review of Educational Research.* Vol 63, No 1 pp. 69–94.

Bartch, J. (1992) An alternative to Spelling: An integrated approach. *Language Arts.* Vol 69, No 6, pp. 404–408.

Bateman, D. and Zidonis, F. (1966) The Effect of a Study of Transformational Grammar on the Writing of Ninth and Tenth Graders. *NCTE Research Report* No. 6. The National Council of Teachers of English, Urbana, Il.

Bauer, L. (1981) Some of the Reasons Why. *Education.* Vol 30, No 4, pp. 14–15.

Bereiter, C. and Scardamalia, M. (1982) From Conversation to Composition: The Role of Instruction in a Developmental Process. In Glaser, R. (ed.) *Advances in Instructional Psychology.* Lawrence Erlbaum, Hillsdale, N.J.

Bereiter, C. and Scardamalia, M. (1983) Does Learning to Write have to be so Difficult? In Freedman, A., Pringle, I. and Yalden, J. (eds) *Learning to Write: First language/Second language.* Longman, London.

Berwick-Emms, P. (1989) Classroom patterns of interaction and their underlying structure: A study of how achievement in the first year of school is influenced by home patterns of interaction. Unpublished Ph.D. Thesis. Christchurch, University of Canterbury.

Bolter, D. (1991) *Writing Space: The Computer, Hypertext, and the History of Writing.* Lawrence Erlbaum Associates, New Jersey.

Braddock R., Lloyd-Jones R. and Schoer, L. (1963) *Research in Written Composition.* The National Council of Teachers of English, Urbana, Ill.

Brann, B. (1996) Spelling Instruction in Primary Schools. *Set* 1, 1–4. New Zealand Council for Educational Research, Wellington, New Zealand.

Bratcher, S. (1994) *Evaluating Children's Writing.* St Martin's Press, New York.

Breen-Williams, A-M. (1992) *Emphasis on message or surface features in young children's writing.* M.Ed. Thesis, University of Canterbury.

Britton, J. (1983) Shaping at the Point of Utterance. In A. Freedman, I. Pringle and J. Yaldin, (Eds) *Learning to Write; First Language/Second Language.* London, Longman.

Bruce, B. and Rubin, A. (1993) *Electronic Quills – A Situated Evaluation of Using Computers for Writing In Classrooms.* Lawrence Erlbaum Associates, New Jersey.

Bruner, J. (1986) *Actual Minds, Possible Worlds.* Harvard University Press, Boston.

Calkins, L. (1986) *The Art of Teaching Writing.* Heinemann, Portsmouth.

Cambourne, B. (1988) *The Whole Story: Natural Learning and the Acquisition of Literacy in the Classroom.* Ashton Scholastic, Gosford, NSW.

Cambourne, B. (1995) Toward an Educationally Relevant Theory of Literacy Learning: Twenty Years of Inquiry. *Reading Teacher.* Vol 49, No 3, pp. 182–190.

Cambourne, B. and Turbill, J. (1987) *Coping with Chaos.* Primary English Teaching Association, Rozelle, NSW.

Cambourne, B. and Turbill, J. (1990) Assessment in Whole-Language Classrooms: Theory into Practice. *The Elementary School Journal.* Vol 90, No 3, pp. 337–349.

Cameron, M., Depree, H., Walker, J. and Moore, D. (1991) Paired Writing: Helping Beginning Writers Get Started. *Set* 5 (2). New Zealand Council for Educational Research, Wellington, NZ.

Carlin, E. (1985) Writing Development: Theory and Practice. Paper presented at International Writing Convention, University of East Anglia, United Kingdom.

Church, R.J. (1990) The use of within-subject designs to measure teh effects of teaching on learning. Paper presented at Conference of New Zealand Association of Research in Education, December 1990.

Clarke, L. (1988) Encouraging Invented Spelling in Grade 1 Writing. *Research in the Teaching of English.* Vol 22, pp. 281–309.

Clay, M. (1975) *What Did I Write?* Heinemann, Auckland.

Clay, M. (1987) *Writing Begins at Home.* Heinemann, Auckland.

Cochrane-Smith, M. (1991) Word Processing and Writing in Elementary Classrooms: A Critical Review of Related Literature. *Review of Educational Research.* Vol 61, No 1, pp. 107–155.

Courtis, S.A. (1949) Rate of Growth Makes a Difference. *Phi Delta Kappa.* Vol 30, pp. 316–323.

Croft, A.C. (1983) *Spell-Write: An Aid to Writing, Spelling and Word Study.* New Zealand Council for Educational Research, Wellington, New Zealand.

Croft, A.C. (1983) *Teachers' Manual for Spell-Write*. New Zealand Council for Educational Research, Wellington.

DeAth, P. (1984) *Spelling Proficiency – An Investigation*. Education Department, University of Canterbury, Christchurch.

Delpit, L. (1988) The Silenced Dialogue: Power and Pedagogy in Education of Other People's Children. *Harvard Education Review*. Vol 58, No 3, pp. 280–298.

Diederich, P. (1974) *Measuring Growth in English*. National Council of Teachers of English, Champaign Urbana, Ill.

Dudley-Marling, C. (1995) Uncertainty and the Whole Language Teacher. *Language Arts*. Vol 72, (4) pp. 252–258.

Duthie, C. (1994) NonFiction: A Genre Study for the Primary Classroom. *Language Arts*. Vol 71 (8), pp. 588–595.

Dyson, A. (1983) The Role of Oral Language in Early Writing Processes. *Research in the Teaching of English*. Vol 17, No 1, pp. 1–30.

Eggleton, J.M. and Windsor, J. (1995) *Linking the Language Strands*. Wings Publication, Auckland.

Elley, W.B. (1985) *Lessons Learned about LARIC*. Education Department, University of Canterbury, Christchurch.

Elley, W.B. (1991) Acquiring Literacy in a Second Language: The Effect of Book-Based Programs. *Language Learning*. Vol 41, No 3, pp. 375–411.

Elley, W.B., Barham, I., Lamb, H. and Wyllie, M. (1975) The Role of Grammar in the Secondary School English Curriculum. *New Zealand Journal of Educational Studies*. Vol 10, pp. 26–42. Reprinted 1976 in *Research in the Teaching of English*. Vol 10, pp. 5–21.

Elley, W.B., Barham, I., Lamb, H. and Wyllie, M. (1979) *The Role of Grammar in a Secondary School Curriculum*. New Zealand Council for Educational Research, Wellington, New Zealand.

Ferritor, D.E., Buckholdt, F., Hamblin, R.L. and Smith, L. (1972) The Effects of Contingent Reinforcement for Attending Behaviour on Work Accomplished. *Journal of Applied Behaviour Analysis*. Vol 5, pp. 7–17.

Fitzgerald, J. (1988) Helping Young Writers to Revise: A Brief Review for Teachers. *The Reading Teacher*. Vol 42 (2), pp. 124–130.

Fitzgerald, J. and Stamm, C. (1992) Variation in Writing Conference Influence on Revision: Two Cases. *Journal of Reading Behaviour*. Vol XXIV (1), pp. 21–50.

Flower, L. and Hayes, J. (1981) A Cognitive Process Theory of Writing. *College Composition and Communication*. Vol 32, pp. 365–386.

Flower, L. and Hayes, J. (1984) Images, Plans and Prose. The Representation of Meaning in Writing. *Written Communication*. Vol 1, No 1, pp. 120–160.

Ford C. (1955) Attitudes of Canterbury Pupils to Written Composition. Research Paper. Education Department. University of Canterbury.

Fortescue, C. (1994) Using Oral and Written Language to Increase Understanding of Math Concepts. *Language Arts*. Vol 71 (8), pp. 576–580.

Freedman, A. (1993) Show and Tell? The Role of Explicit Teaching in the Learning of New Genres. *Research in the Teaching of English*. Vol 27 (3).

Freyberg, P. (1964) A Comparison of Two Approaches to the Teaching of Spelling. *British Journal of Educational Psychology*. Vol 34, pp. 178–186.

Gentry, R. (1982) Spelling Genius at Work. *The Reading Teacher*. Vol 36, No 2, pp. 192–199.

Glynn, E., McNaughton, S. and Wotherspoon, A. (1975) Modification of Reading, Writing and Attending Behaviour in a Special Class for Retarded Children. Unpublished Research Paper, Department of Education, University of Auckland.

Glynn, T., Crooks, T., Bethune, N., Ballard, K. and Smith, J. (1989) *Reading Recovery in Context*. Report to Research and Statistics Division, New Zealand Department of Education.

Goodridge, M. and McNaughton, S. (1993) The Co-Construction of Writing Expertise in Family Activity. Paper presented at the 15th Annual Conference of the New Zealand Association for Research in Education, Hamilton.

Gordon, E. (1991) Grammar Teaching in New Zealand Schools: the Past, the Present and the Future. *English in Aotearoa*. No 15, pp. 19–24.

Gordon, I. (1947) *The Teaching of English*. New Zealand Council for Educational Research, Wellington, New Zealand.

Gorman, T.P., White, J., Brooks, G., Maclure, M. and Kispal, A. (1988) *Language Performance in Schools: Review of APU Language Monitoring*. 1979–83. Department of Education & Science, London, UK.

Graves, Donald H. (1979) What Children Show Us about Revision. *Language Arts*. 56 (3), pp. 312–319.

Graves, Donald H. (1983) *Writing: Teachers & Children at Work*. Heinemann Educational Books, Exeter, NH.

Graves, Donald H. (1994) *A Fresh Look at Writing*. Heinneman, Portsmouth, NH.

Hammill, D. Larsen, S. and McNutt, G. (1977) The Effect of Spelling Instruction: A preliminary study. *Elementary School Journal*. Vol 78, pp. 67–72.

Harpin, W. (1976) *The Second R: Writing Development in the Junior School*. Unwin Education, London.

Harris, R. (1962) An Experimental Inquiry into the Functions and Value of Formal Grammar in the Teaching of English. Ph.D. dissertation, University of London.

Hartwell, P. (1985) Grammar, Grammars and the Teaching of Grammar. *College English*. Vol 47, No 2, pp. 105–127.

Hayes, J. and Flower, L. (1980) Identifying the Organization of Writing Process. In Gregg, L. and Steinberg, E. (1980) *Cognitive Processes in Writing*. Lawrence Erlbaum, New Jersey.

Heath, S. (1983) *Ways with Words*. Cambridge, Cambridge University Press.

Heenan, J. (1986) *Writing: Process and Product*. Auckland, Longman Paul.

Hillocks, G. (1984) What Works in Teaching Composition: A Meta-Analysis of Experimental Treatment Studies. *American Journal of Education*. No 93, pp. 133–170.

Hillocks, G. (1986) *Research on Written Composition*. ERIC Clearing House on Reading and Communication Skills, Urbana, Il.

Hood, H. (1994) The Great Writing Debate – Why the Fuss about 'Genre'? *New Zealand Principal*. April.

Hood, H. (1995) *Left to Write*. Berkeley Publishing, Auckland.

Hopman, M. and Glynn, T. (1989) The Effect of Correspondence Training on the Rate and Quality of Expression of Four Low-Achieving Boys. *Educational Psychology*. Vol 9, pp. 197–213.

Hunt, K. (1965) *Grammatical Structures Written at Three Grade Levels*. Research No 3. National Council of Teaching of English, Illinois.

Jerram, H., Glynn, T. and Tuck, B. (1988) Responding to the Message: Providing a Social Context for Children Learning to Write. *Educational Psychology*. Vol 8, pp. 31–40.

Kepner, C. (1991) An Experiment in the Relationship of Types of Written Feedback to the Development of Second-Language Writing Skills. *The Modern Language Journal*. Vol 75, pp. 305–313.

Krashen, S. (1991) Bilingual Education: A Focus on Current Research. *Focus*. No 3, Spring.

Krashen, S. (1994) The Pleasure Hypothesis. In Alatis, J. (ed.) *Educational Linguistics, Cross-Cultural Communication and Global Interdependence*. Georgetown University Press, Washington DC.

Kress, G. (1994) *Learning to Write*. Routledge, London.

Kroll, B.M. and Schafer, J.C. (1977) *The Development of Error Analysis and its Implications for the Teaching of Composition*. Paper presented at Conference on College Composition, Kansas City, Missouri.

Kroll, L.R. (1991) *Making Meaning: Longitudinal Aspects of Learning to Write*. Paper presented at the Annual Meeting of the American Psychological Association, 1991. ERIC document.

Lamb, H. (1987) *Writing Performance in New Zealand Schools*. Department of Education, Wellington, New Zealand.

Langley, J. (1994) An Analysis of One Child's Emergent Writing. Unpublished paper, Dunedin College of Education, Dunedin.

Lensmire, T.J. (1994a) Writing Workshop as Carnival: Reflections on an Alternative Learning Environment. *Harvard Educational Review*. Vol 64 (4) pp. 371–391.

Lensmire, T.J. (1994b) *When Children Write: Critical Re-Visions of the Writing Workshop*. Teachers College Press, New York.

Loban, W. (1976) *Language Development, Kindergarten through Grade 12*. Research Report No 18, NCTE Illinois.

Logan, B. and Glynn, T. (1989) Responding in Writing: Improving Children's Writing through Responsive Written Feedback. Unpublished Manuscript, Education Department, University of Otago, Dunedin.

Manolakes, G. (1975) Teaching of Spelling; a Pilot Study. *Elementary English*. Vol 52, pp. 243–247.

McNaughton, S. (1994) Why there might be Several Ways to Read Storybooks to Preschoolers in Aotearoa/New Zealand: Models of Tutoring and Sociocultural Diversity in how Families Read Books to Preschoolers. In M. Kohl de Oliveria and J. Valsinor (eds) *Literacy in Human Development*. Ablex, Norwood, NJ.

McNaughton, S. (1995) *Patterns of Emergent Literacy: Processes of Development and Transition*. Oxford University Press, Auckland.

McNaughton, S., Parr, J. and Smith, L.T. (1996) *Processes of Teaching and Learning in Literacy – Writing*. Final Report to Ministry of Education. Research Project No ER35/5335, Ministry of Eduction, Wellington.

Manning, M. et al. (1990) Writing Development of Inner City Primary Students: Comparative Effects of a Whole Language and a Skills-Oriented Program. *Paper presented at the Annual Meeting of the Mid-South Educational Research Association*. ERIC document, New Orleans.

Marholin, D. and Steinman, W. (1977) Stimulus Control in the Classroom as a Function of Behaviour Reinforced. *Journal of Applied Behaviour Analysis*. Vol 10, pp. 465–478.

Meckel, H. (1963) Research on Teaching Composition and Literature. In Gage N. (ed.) *Handbook of Research on Teaching*. Rand McNally, Chicago, Il.

Miller, G. (1977) *Spontaneous Apprentices: Children and Language*. Seabury, New York.

Ministry of Education (1992) *Dancing with the Pen*. Learning Media, Wellington.

Moll, L. (1990) *Vygotsky and Education: Instructional Implications and Applications of Sociohistorical Psychology*. Cambridge, Cambridge University Press.

Monteith, S. (1991) Writing Process versus Traditional Writing Classrooms: Writing Ability and Attitudes of Second Grade Students. *Paper presented at the Annual Meeting of the Mid-South Educational Research Association*, Lexington. ERIC document.

NAEP (1990) *The Writing Report Card 1984–88*. Educational Testing Service, Princeton, New Jersey.

Ninio, A. and Bruner, J. (1978) The Achievements and Antecedents of Labelling. *Journal of Child Language*. No 5, pp. 5–15.

Olson, M. and Raffeld, P. (1987) The Effects of Written Comments on the Quality of Student Compositions and the Learning of Content. *Reading Psychology*. Vol 8, pp. 273–293.

Perera, K. (1994) *Children's Writing and Reading*. Oxford, Basil Blackwell.

Peters, M. (1985) *Spelling: Caught or Taught*. Routledge, London.

Philips, D. (1982) Evaluating Writing. *Set* No 1, Item 13. New Zealand Council for Educational Research, Wellington.

Philips, D. (1985) *A Month's Writing in Four Classrooms*. New Zealand Council for Educational Research, Wellington.

Pitman, J. and St. John, J. (1969) *Alphabets and Reading*. New York. Pitman.

Purves, A.C. (1990) *The Scribal Society*. Longman, New York.

Radebaugh, M. (1985) Children's Perceptions of their Spelling Strategies. *The Reading Teacher*. Vol 38, No 6, pp. 532–536.

Rapeer, L. (1913) The Problem of Formal Grammar in Elementary Education. *Journal of Educational Psychology.* Vol 4, pp. 125–137.

Rinsland, H.D. (1945) *A Basic Writing Vocabulary of Elementary School Children.* Macmillan, New York.

Roberts, K. and Ehri, L. (1983) Effects of Two Types of Letter Rehearsal on Word Memory in Skilled and Less Skilled Beginning Readers. *Contemporary Educational Psychology.* Vol 8, pp. 375–390.

Rumsey, I. and Ballard, K. (1985) Teaching Self-Management Strategies for Independent Story Writing to Children with Classroom Behaviour Difficulties. *Educational Psychology.* Vol 5, pp. 147–157.

Sacks, O. (1995) *An Anthropologist on Mars.* Picador, Sydney.

Scardamalia, M. and Bereiter, C. (1986) Research in Written Composition in Wittrock, M. (ed.) *Handbook of Research on Teaching.* 3rd edition, American Educational Research Association, MacMillan, New York.

Scardamalia, M., Bereiter, C. and Lamon, M. (1994) The CISLE Project: Trying to Bring the Classroom into the World 3. In K. McGilly (ed.) *Classroom Lessons: Integrating Cognitive Theory and Classroom Practice.* pp. 210–228. Bradford/MIT, Cambridge, MA.

Schonell, F. (1949) *Essentials in Teaching and Testing Spelling.* MacMillan, London.

Scriven, J. and Glynn, T. (1983) Performance Feedback on Written Tasks for Low Achieving Secondary Students. *New Zealand Journal of Educational Studies.* Vol 18, pp. 134–145.

Semeke, H. (1989) Effects of the Red Pen. *Foreign Language Annals.* Vol 17, pp. 195–202.

Shepherd, K. (1992) Two Feedback Systems. Do they Make a Difference? *Relc Journal.* Vol 23, pp. 103–110.

Shook, S., Marrion, L. and Ollila, L. (1989) Primary Children's Concepts About Writing. *Journal of Educational Research.* Vol 28 (3), pp. 133–138.

Silberman, A. (1991) *Growing up Writing. Teaching our Children to Write, Think and Learn.* 1st paperback edition, Heinemann, Portsmouth.

Smith, F. (1982) *Writing and the Writer.* Heinemann, London.

Smith, F. (1988) *Joining the Literacy Club.* London, Heinemann.

Snyder, I. (1993) Writing with Word Processors: a Research Overview. *Educational Research.* Vol 35, No 1, pp. 49–69.

Spiegal, L., Andrews, S. and Hoover, J. (1994) Rural and Small Town Teachers' Self Reported Use of Written Expression. *Rural Educator.* Vol 16, (1).

Spencer, E. (1983) *Writing Matters Across the Curriculum.* Scottish Council for Research in Education, Edinburgh.

Stahl, S., Pagnucco, J. and Suttles, C. (1996) First Graders' Reading and Writing Instruction in Traditional and Process-Oriented Classes. *Journal of Educational Research.* Vol 89, (3), pp. 131–144.

Stotsky, S. (1995) The Uses and Limitations of Personal or Personalized Writing in Writing Theory, Research, and Instruction. *Reading Research Quarterly.* Vol 30, (4), pp. 758–776.

Stubbs, M. (1980) *Language and Literacy: The Sociolinguistics of Reading and Writing.* Routledge & Keegan Paul, London.

Swarbrick, S. (1989) *The Impact of Process Writing on Children's Language.* Education Department, University of Canterbury Research. Report No 89–2. Christchurch, New Zealand.

Tharp, R. and Gallimore, R. (1988) *Rousing Minds to Life: Teaching, Learning and School in Social Context.* Cambridge University Press, Cambridge.

Thorstad, G. (1991) The Effect of Orthography on the Acquisition of Literacy Skills. *British Journal of Psychology.* Vol 82, pp. 527–537.

Tizard, B. and Hughes, B. (1984) *Young Children Learning: Talking and Thinking at Home and at School.* Fontana, London.

Tomlinson, D. (1994) Errors in the Research into the Effectiveness of Grammar Teaching. *English in Education.* Vol 28, No 1, pp. 20–26.

Tough, J. (1974) *Focus on Meaning: Talking to some Purpose with Young Children.* Unwin, London.

Van de Gein, R. (1991) *A Study of the Effects of Grammar Instruction on Junior Writing.* University of Amsterdam, Centre for Educational Research, Amsterdam.

Varble, E. (1990) Analysis of Writing Samples of Students Taught by Teachers Using Whole Language and Traditional Approaches. *Journal of Educational Research.* Vol 83, No 5, pp. 245–251.

Vygotsky, L. (1962) *Thought and Language.* MIT Press, Cambridge.

Walker, A. (1988) Writing – across the Curriculum: The Second Decade. *English Quarterly.* Vol 21, (2), pp. 93–108.

Walker, C. and Elias, D (1987) Writing Conference Talk: Factors Associated with High- and Low-Rated Writing Conferences. *Research in the Teaching of English.* Vol 21, (3), pp. 266–285.

Walmsley, S.A. and Adams E.L. (1993) Realities of 'Whole Language'. *Language Arts.* Vol 70, (3), pp. 272–282.

Ward, R. (ed.) (1992) *Readings about Writing.* Dunmore Press, Palmerston North.

Weiner, S. (1994) Four First Graders' Descriptions of How they Spell. *Elementary School Journal.* Vol 94, (3), pp. 315–331.

Wells, G. (1986) The Meaning Makers: Children *Learning Language and using Language to Learn.* Heinemann, Portsmouth.

Western Australian Education Department (1994) *Writing Developmental Continuum.* Perth, Longman.

Wheldall, K. and Glynn, T. (1989) *Effective Classroom Learning.* Basil Blackwell, Oxford.

Wilde, S. (1990) A Proposal for a New Spelling Curriculum. *The Elementary School Journal.* Vol 90, No 3, pp. 275–290.

Willinsky, J. (1990) *The New Literacy: Redefining Reading and Writing in the School.* Routledge, New York.

Wilson, M. and Glynn, T. (1983) Increasing Self-Selection and Self-Location of Words by Mildly Retarded Children During Story Writing. *The Exceptional Child.* Vol 30, pp. 210–220.

Winograd, K. (1993) Selected Writing Behaviors of Fifth Graders As They Compose Original Mathematics Story Problems. *Research in the Teaching of English.* Vol 27, (4), pp. 369–394.

Winograd, K. and Higgens, K. (1995) Writing, Reading, and Talking Mathematics: One Interdisciplinary Possiblity. *The Reading Teacher.* Vol 48, (4), pp. 310–317.

Index